Working in an Hotel

Working in an HOTEL

MICHAEL J BOELLA
MHCIMA, MIPM, AMBIM

B T Batsford Limited
London

First published 1979
ISBN 0 7134 1138 4

Filmset by Progress Filmsetting, London
Printed in Great Britain by
Redwood Burn Ltd, Trowbridge, Wilts
for the publishers, B T Batsford Limited
4 Fitzhardinge Street, London W1H 0AH

For Jonathan and Elena
and
everyone who has to choose a career

Contents

Acknowledgment

It is right and proper for the author of a book of this nature to thank those who have contributed to its contents. As is usual however, when a book draws upon the experience of a lifetime, all of those who have contributed would be too numerous to name personally.

However, I should like to thank the following people for making a particular contribution. Professor John Fuller for suggesting me to the publisher, as the author of this book, Brian Carroll, Derek Bailey, Nick Patterson and the directors of Crest Hotels, Diane Wood of Grand Metropolitan. Henry Edwards, Brian Worthington, Giles Jackman and Mike Foren of Centre Hotels. Miles Quest of Catering Times, and also the following organisations for their permission to use material such as job descriptions, menus, wine lists and photographs, or for checking the facts. Any errors however, are my own responsibility:

The British Hotels, Restaurants and Caterers Association.
The City and Guilds of London Institute.
The Hotel, Catering and Institutional Management Association.
The Hotel and Catering Industry Training Board.
The Catering Times.
Crest Hotels Europe.

Finally Liz Cullen for her work on the typescript.

The professionals in the industry and the professional critics, I would ask to bear with me if in some cases I have over-simplified a description. This is because I have very clearly in mind the young reader to whom I wish to convey as clear a picture as possible of the industry in general.

MJB
Westwood
1979

Illustrations

The photographs between pages 48 and 49 are reproduced by kind permission of the Hotel and Catering Industry Training Board to which Organisation both author and publisher offer their grateful thanks.

Preface

Each year many thousands of young people are faced with the formidable task of choosing a career. In the past many followed in the footsteps of their parents, whether or not they were equipped to follow that particular path. Even today this still occurs, but thankfully, more people now have the opportunity of thinking much more carefully about their choice of career.

Today modern technological change means that many industries face drastic change and often redundancies as well. The career decisions taken now must therefore take into account the economic and social conditions that are likely to exist in the years to come. So that anyone making a choice must consider which trades, industries and profession will be in demand in the future.

There is little doubt, a world disaster apart, that there will be an ever-increasing demand for every aspect of travel, leisure and hotel services—that is, the tourist industry. Consequently, everyone who has to make a career choice, or who has to give advice to those making such a choice, must consider seriously this industry, of which hotels are a major and essential part.

For most of its history, the hotel industry in Britain has been bedevilled by a reputation that has deterred many from making their careers in hotels. Some of the reputation was deserved. Much was not. But in any event there are big changes afoot within the hotel industry which undoubtedly make it a very serious consideration for everyone with the right personality. I hope that this book will make it easier for people to come to a better understanding of the industry when considering what career to follow.

Having written this book it occurred to me that because it sets out to describe the industry in simple terms for those knowing little or nothing about hotels this book may also be of value to students just embarking upon their studies.

Students taking Ordinary National Diploma or some of the City and Guilds courses may find it useful as an introductory text.

An introduction to the world of hotels

Choosing a career, a few years ago, was something that depended to a great extent upon luck and one's personal circumstances. Unless your parents were perceptive and your teachers well informed the chances of your making a career choice to suit your own particular personality were minimal. Today however things have improved with a whole range of expert advice available to the young person about to make what will be the most important decision in life – the choice of career.

Are you the right type of person?

Before making that decision, however, you will need to know something about yourself. Obviously because you are reading this book you are thinking about your future career and specifically you are considering hotels as a possibility. Hotel work makes special demands upon its work people and unless you are prepared to meet these demands fully you will not find the industry rewarding and, worse still, you will not find it enjoyable.

I will, therefore, describe the type of person I believe the industry welcomes and if you fit the description you should read on. If, on the other hand you do not fit the bill, I believe you would be well advised to consider other careers. The hotel industry, along with some others, is a particularly demanding one and life for those who are not entirely suited to it will be very unrewarding, even miserable.

High days and holidays

Before anything else you must recognise that hotels work when their guests are resting from work, so you will have to expect to work some evenings, weekends and during 'bank holidays'. The busiest time for many hotels is during the summer holiday season so many hotel staff have to take their own holidays out of season.

On the other hand, many people find this an advantage. They are able to take their own time off when others are working so shops, restaurants and holiday resorts are not crowded.

Working for other people's comfort and entertainment

Secondly, hotels exist because they satisfy people's needs for rest, food and entertainment. This means that everyone in an hotel is working for other people so unless you enjoy other people's company and, more importantly, unless you see working for other people as personally satisfying then hotels are not for you.

Thirdly, because in hotels you work for other people much of the work cannot be postponed until tomorrow. If guests do not have their dinner when they want it they cannot wait a day or two for it. And if 'knocking off' time comes half way through someone's meal you cannot leave. You have to finish your work before 'knocking off'.

Self-discipline

Fourthly, even in the largest hotels, there are few, if any staff, who work under the amount of supervision common in many other industries. A hotel consists of many departments, each responsible for a part of the service to the guest. Often these departments will be 'manned' by only one person and he or she will be entirely responsible, without supervision, for providing service to guests. A sense of responsibility and self-discipline is therefore essential.

Never a dull day

Finally, because hotels are a place for people to eat, sleep, work, play, relax and entertain in, everything that happens in ordinary life occurs in hotels. Most days will be reasonably routine, insofar as dealing with the individual wants of maybe hundreds of guests, can be routine. On other occasions, however, a day in an hotel will bring experiences which test the resilience, nerve, and sense of humour of the best.

Dealing with irate guests, lost room keys and lost, sometimes stolen property, bomb hoaxes and false fire alarms are all in the daily routine.

Recognising guests who intend to leave without paying, or who intend to strip a room of every movable item is another talent that grows in time. And to clear up the occasional filth and mess left by a guest is something else to which the staff have to become accustomed.

Some occurrences are funny, some are sad, some are tragic and distressing like the occasional death, or suicide, that happens from time to time in hotels. At a more dramatic level, hotel staff may be involved in news which makes the head-lines, such as international or national political events.

Often too, hotel staff will be party to events long before the general public. Exhibitions and the launching of new products often take place under a cloak of secrecy within hotels and the hotel staff are expected to treat such occurrences with the same discretion as they treat every one of their guests' idiosyncrasies and peccadilloes.

The great and the famous use hotels and everyone employed in an hotel will meet and look after people that he or she would never have imagined being able to meet in normal circumstances. Pop stars, well known sportsmen, politicians, business leaders, trade union leaders, broadcasters, are all part of the life of hotels, particularly those in city centres.

Now if you still feel that the hotel industry is for you what are your prospects likely to be?

Prospects – plenty more room for hotels

To start with, because the industry serves our basic needs for food and shelter, and because people will continue to travel away from home, there will always be a need for hotels. Also, as each year goes by, more people acquire the means to travel, consequently tourism, of which hotels are a vital part, is now considered to be one of the world's most important growth industries. In Great Britain, for example, it is expected that the total number of tourist nights (ie a night spent away from home for pleasure or business) will have increased by nearly 30 per cent between 1973 and 1985, the majority of this increase taking place between 1980 and 1985. In order to cope with their share of this total demand it is expected that the hotel industry will have to increase its numbers of bedrooms by about 65 000. Some of these new rooms will be built onto existing hotels whilst others will be in new hotels. It is anticipated that about a quarter of these new hotels will be required in traditional holiday areas, about a quarter in urban areas and the remainder in London. Most of all this new investment in hotels is likely to be in the less expensive type of hotel.

Prospects for employment therefore are good, with a steady

growth to the industry. It is vitally important, however, in considering long term career prospects, to consider what alternative employment there is should one's first choice industry go through hard times, or if the first choice does not work out as you hoped.

Plenty of alternative jobs

This in fact, is one of the strongest points in favour of choosing a career in hotels because many of the jobs and skills are very transferable to other fields. Skilled cooks, for example, can work not only in hotels but also in restaurants, hospitals, schools, universities, office blocks, factories and even in the North Sea on oil rigs. And this transferability is not confined to the British Isles because well trained and skilled staff in the hotel and catering industry are needed throughout the world. British companies such as Trust Houses Forte and Grand Metropolitan run hotels in many countries overseas including countries as far away as Hong Kong, Australia, Africa and the United States. Once again, employment with one of these companies need not confine you to hotels because they run a variety of subsidiary companies which specialise in such things as industrial catering, motorway restaurants and even 'in-flight' catering for airlines.

What type of job?

If you decide to make the hotel industry your career what type of job could you choose? The answer to that question is that the range of choice is considerable. The largest hotels can accommodate many hundreds of people in the bedrooms alone and if they have restaurants, bars and large banqueting facilities they accommodate hundreds more. So if you include staff it is possible for there to be well over two thousand people in a hotel at one time. This is equivalent to a sizeable little town and, as in a town, you can find most trades and occupations. Apart from the most obvious jobs you would expect to find in a hotel such as receptionists, roommaids and waiters there are many others. These include clerks and secretaries, florists and musicians, carpenters and painters, laundry men and linen maids, electricians and porters, even house detectives and doctors.

Many of these jobs have specialised training which is not unique to hotels, florists and electricians are two examples but in this book only those jobs which are specific to hotels or the hotel and catering industry are dealt with in any detail.

Before that however it is important for you to consider if you join the industry who or what type of organisation you are likely to work for.

What type of employer?

Here again the industry has considerable variety to offer. At one end of the scale are hotel companies which own and run some of the world's largest and best hotels here and overseas. These include Trust Houses Forte who run such famous hotels as the Grosvenor House in Park Lane London and the Georges V in the centre of Paris. Grand Metropolitan likewise run large and famous hotels such as the Piccadilly and the Brittania in the West End of London.

Apart from these famous hotels such companies also run many other hotels, some large, some famous but most are the many less glamorous and smaller hotels wherever the Companies feel there is a need for the services of an hotel.

Brewery Hotels

After companies such as these are the hotel companies run by the famous breweries. These include such hotel companies as Crest of Bass Charrington with seventy hotels here and in Europe, Embassy Hotels of Allied Breweries, and Thistle of Scottish and Newcastle Breweries. Many of the smaller regional breweries likewise have their hotel subsidiaries and these include such companies as Swallow Hotels of Vaux Breweries and Red Rose Hotels of Greenall Whitley.

Apart from their larger hotels many of the brewery companies' public houses have letting bedrooms and restaurants and so can be described as hotels. If these smaller hotels are taken into account the brewery companies are without doubt the largest single group of hotel operators in the country.

Conglomerates

Apart from the Companies which have always been involved in hotels and catering are other companies who invest in a whole range of different businesses including hotels. These are the conglomerates and these include the Imperial Company (known mainly for cigarettes) who own Courage Breweries, who in turn own Acorn Hotels.

Other companies in the hotel business are those companies which invest in leisure such as the Coral Group which owns Centre Hotels a company which runs hotels in England and Scotland, and other parts of the world such as Holland, the Seychelles Islands and Africa.

Where to start

Most people who train formally for the industry, that is, take a recognised course, will probably start their career with one of these larger companies. However, one of the great attractions of the hotel industry is that it also provides plenty of opportunity to work in smaller and privately owned hotels for those who may not wish to work in a large company. In fact although there are many quite large companies involved in hotels it is estimated that the top twenty hotel companies own only 5 per cent of the hotels and 15 per cent of the bedrooms. The top two companies between them own only 5 per cent of the country's estimated half million bedrooms. The majority of hotels are small, unlicensed and independently owned. This fact not only means that the range of employers in the industry is considerable but it also means that there are plenty of opportunities for people to set up in business on their own, with only limited capital.

Whilst hotel keeping is without doubt one of the world's oldest industries because of the influence of many different factors it is becoming a very sophisticated one. The larger companies all rely on highly specialised staff to look after many different parts of the business. There are accountants, computer experts, personnel and industrial relations experts, sales and marketing people amongst the many different specialists needed to run a modern hotel business.

What about conditions?

Anyone considering making hotel work a career is bound to hear reports about low pay, long hours and high labour turnover. In many cases this reputation is well deserved, but in many others such reports are based upon insufficient information.

Pay and other benefits

Whilst it is true that the actual pay many employees receive appears low when compared to other industries, the value of fringe benefits is either ignored completely, or grossly undervalued.

Most hotel staff have most, if not all of their meals provided free of charge, and for 'living-in' staff there are no household bills, such as gas and electricity, to pay. Nor are there bus fares or petrol costs in order to get to work. Many employees are provided with uniform, and even personal laundry may be paid for by the employer. Consequently, for 'living-in' staff wages need not be spent on many of the living expenses accepted by other people as a normal part of the cost of living.

For a manager who is expected by his employer to 'live-in', these benefits generally extend to his wife and family as well. So, many of the industry's managers too are largely protected from inflation because it is the employer who has to cope with price increases for electricity and gas, fares and petrol, wear and tear and so on.

Service charges and tips

In addition to ordinary wages, many staff earn extra in the form of tips, and in some cases a share of the service charge made by most hotels.

Service charges The service charge is often a cause of trouble because most guests and many staff think that the service charge is automatically distributed to the staff. In some cases, this is so, the service charge is distributed amongst the staff. In others, however, the service charge is another means of the owner raising extra revenue, which is not distributed directly to the staff although in some cases staff will receive higher basic wages than their colleagues who receive a direct share of the service charge or tips.

Tips and the 'tronc' system Tipping has always been a major source of grievance between staff and staff, staff and guests and staff and management. Tips take two main forms. There are those hotels or even departments who allow staff to keep their own tips whilst in other cases, the tips will be pooled into a 'tronc' and then distributed generally on a seniority basis. Some people would like to see tipping eliminated, and some companies have gone a long way to eliminating it, but there is little doubt that tipping will remain in the industry.

Other fringe benefits

Apart from these benefits, there are many other benefits resulting from the key role played by many hotels in the life of the local community. Many hotel managers and their staff receive free tickets to the local cinemas, discotheques and theatres. Guests such as exhibition organisers, frequently leave presents for the staff, which in normal retail terms can be worth many pounds.

The benefits that hotel staff can receive can be worth little or they can be worth a great deal. At the extreme, there are hotel employees who even keep horses on the hotel grounds at no expense. However, for a young person starting a job it must be remembered that whilst tips and other benefits may be attractive, a basic low rate of pay will present problems in obtaining mortgages and the like and whilst free meals and tickets may be attractive money and the freedom to spend it how you wish may be more attractive.

Hours of work

Likewise with hours, one hears constantly that hours are long and inconvenient, but the truth is that actual hours worked are little different to the national average. The problem is how the hours are spread over the average day. For many people working in hotels, the average day is organised around breakfast time and lunch time, tea-time and dinner times, and arrival and departure times. The consequence is that there are spells when many staff are needed and other times when hardly anyone is needed. As a result, people work what is called the 'split shift', that is working for two or three spells separated by time off. So whilst the total hours of work may only amount to seven or eight hours these may be spread over as many as fifteen or sixteen in a working day.

For some, particular family people, this will obviously be very inconvenient or unsatisfactory. For others, however and especially single people in holiday resorts this arrangement can mean being free every afternoon to meet friends, to go to the beach or to go riding or sailing or to do whatever else appeals.

The Wages Council

Some of the conditions of employment such as minimum pay and hours, and holiday entitlements are determined by a Wages Council which has both employer and employee representation.

The Wages Council is concerned only with minimum rates of pay and in many cases, probably in most cases, individuals negotiate contracts which are above the minimum rates of pay.

Holidays

Currently, the holiday entitlement is seventeen working days per annum. For many, because of the seasonal nature of hotel work, some of this might be taken out of season. Additionally, some employers are pleased for their staff to take extra unpaid holiday during the out of season spell, just after Christmas for example.

Sickness benefits

With regard to sickness benefit schemes, the industry is not particularly generous so far as the formal contracts are concerned. It appears that about half of hotel employees are covered in some way. In practice however, it is likely that many more employees are covered by some form of informal scheme and many managers are getting round, or even entirely ignoring their company policy, particularly, where the longer serving employees are concerned.

Pension schemes

Pension Schemes are certainly not a general thing in hotels. However, some of the larger companies and also some of the more progressive smaller companies have schemes now.

Training

Training, which is obvious of critical interest to readers of this book, varies considerably from hotel to hotel and from company to company. The larger companies generally speaking have well planned schemes for just about every type of person they are likely to employ. How the actual training is implemented however, in the hotels depends upon the individual managers and heads of departments.

In smaller hotels, training can be very good but, as a general rule, they are not the best places to train in for a whole variety of reasons. Firstly, in smaller hotels, there are fewer 'spare' staff to spend time training newcomers. Even the manager, and his assistant (if he has one), will take their turn 'behind the bar', and in the reception. Secondly, larger hotels and larger companies can afford the time and money to send people responsible for training on instructors' courses. And finally, larger companies are more likely to ensure that people who are supposed to be trained are in fact being trained if for no other reason than that they may fall foul of the industrial training board.

Obviously, there are many small hotels who can and do give training which is good, and frequently better than that given by the larger companies. But likewise, there are thousands of small hotels which are not equipped to give any training at all. Consequently, if there is to be a choice between big hotels and small, I would recommend the bigger hotels. And, I would always discover if the company's training schemes have been approved by the Hotel and Catering Industry Training Board.

Management styles

Most people decide to work in hotels mainly because they enjoy meeting people. The types of relationship which exist in hotels therefore are obviously of great importance to people considering hotels as a career. Unfortunately it is of course not possible to generalise and to say that a particular type of working atmosphere is most common. This is because the atmosphere in each hotel will depend upon the owners, the managers, the staff and the customers.

An autocratic manager who does not listen to his staff and does not consider their needs, will create an atmosphere which will be very different to a manager who believes that he will only have satisfied customers if he has satisfied staff.

The key thing however that is common to virtually all hotels is that staff and management are constantly working to tight deadlines; breakfast, lunch, dinner, opening hours, closing time, check out time, room release times. Hotels therefore are consequently working from one peak to the next. Every department has its own peaks followed by quiet spells. The staff in each department have some relief after the peaks but one group of employees, the managers are concerned with all of them. And, like the theatre, it is a very, very rare occasion that these various deadlines are not met. The standards may not always be what the guest or the management want, but the doors open on time, every time.

Team work

An important fact about hotel work is that most departments in an hotel, even in large hotels, have only a few people on duty at one time. The absence of just one creates extra work for those remaining. So the late arrival of a member of staff means that someone else will not finish on time, and if someone is absent it means that a colleague may have to work an unexpected shift, maybe following the one they have just completed. Consequently, a sense of loyalty grows up between many of the key staff which prevents them letting one another down.

This loyalty extends to many of the managers and even to the hotel itself. This may seem a strange statement, but it is a fact that many hotel staff working in hotels owned by the country's biggest companies do not identify themselves in any way with the owning company but only with the hotel and its management, staff and customers. Often when a manager or a head of department leaves one hotel to work in another, he will take several of his staff with him to the new hotel.

What about unions?

For most of their history, the vast majority of hotels have been owned by individual proprietors. Their trade has been seasonal and many of their staff move from hotel to hotel with the change of the seasons. The average hotel has only about twenty five bedrooms, and only a handful of staff. And the country's many thousands of hotels are scattered over the whole map of Great Britain. The staff themselves, partly because of the tipping system, had developed an entrepreneurial attitude to their work which prevented their seeing any benefits of union membership. In fact, they probably saw more disadvantages than advantages.

In the last few years however, a whole variety of things have occurred which appears to be changing the position of unions in the industry. Firstly, and probably most importantly, large companies now own key sections of the industry particulary the large hotels, which are concentrated in numbers in the country's urban centres.

These hotels are managed by professionally trained managers, some of whom have different attitudes to unions from those held by owners of hotels. Equally importantly these larger hotels have succeeded by running conferences and the like, in reducing the seasonal business and employment cycle effects so that there is now more continuity in employment.

A major consequence therefore is an increasing growth of union membership and union influence in the industry. As recently as the early 1970s, it was considered unlikely that most new managers in the industry would encounter union officials, shop stewards or even union members. Today however, the majority of managers in large hotels will be coming into daily contact with unions and their members as a normal matter of course.

Job security

One of the associated trends, has been a radical change in employment and dismissal procedures. A few years ago, the industry had a notorious reputation for thoughtless 'hire and fire' practices. Fortunately, things have improved in this direction with much more formal and responsible procedures being adopted by most of the larger companies at least.

Husbands and wives

Because many hotels, particularly the smaller and medium sized ones, provide accommodation for the manager and his family, hotels attract a high proportion of joint managers, that is, husband and wife teams to share the running of a hotel. The duties of running the hotel are normally split between the two depending upon the skills and preference of each. In some cases, the manager will look after the catering and his wife will look after housekeeping. In other cases, the wife will look after the administration, whilst in yet others it is the wife who supervises the catering with the husband running the bars and administration. Some companies encourage joint management, paying both the husband and wife the going rate for each job. Other companies discourage joint employment refusing to employ a husband and his wife in the same hotel.

In many ways, working together is an attractive arrangement, because without such an arrangement and because of the unusual hours normally worked, husbands and wives would find difficulty spending time together. Admittedly, much of the time together is working together and this can have serious disadvantages. In the smallest hotels, husbands and wives may decide that only one can be off duty at a time. The consequence is that husbands and wives spend little or none of their leisure time together. Broken marriages, as a result, are not uncommon.

Apart from joint management many other married couples can find work together in the same hotel. Living in accommodation, as for single people is provided, and the opportunities, for those who wish to, to save is considerable. One newly married couple, the husband a chef and the wife an assistant housekeeper saved enough in six months working and living in the same hotel, to pay a down payment and to furnish their own home.

Job satisfaction

Most people who have worked for some time in hotels will say that although money is important it is not the main reward they enjoy from their work. They will tell you that hotel work is very varied, no two days are alike. No two guests are alike. They will tell you that most skilled hotel staff enjoy considerable freedom from supervision. A room-maid, for example, may see her boss, a housekeeper only once in a day. For the remainder she is left to get on with her work as she sees fit. Hotel staff will tell you that there is team spirit in most hotels. Although one may be working alone, with little supervision, everything one is doing fits into an overall pattern. The room-maids have to finish their work by a certain hour so that the receptionists can let the rooms to guests as they arrive, rather than keeping guests waiting after a tiring journey. Laundry men and linen maids have to make sure that linen is available for the room-maids and the dining room staff so that they can make the beds and lay the tables before the guests arrive. This may be as simple as changing the bed linen in one bedroom or it may involve laying up tables for a banquet for a thousand guests. No one can slip up in his or her job because colleagues will be let down and so too will the guests.

Finally, many hotel staff will tell you that their greatest satisfaction is knowing that they have brought some satisfaction or pleasure to others. This may be simply making a businessman's stay away from his home and family more comfortable. It may be making an important conference more enjoyable, efficient and successful. Or it could be making a family's annual holiday the most enjoyable event of their year.

A brief history of hotels

There will always be a debate between the hoteliers and restaurateurs about where the best food is to be found — in hotels or in restaurants. Restaurateurs argue that it is the only thing they have to offer so it has to be good. Many hoteliers, on the other hand, argue that because they have guests whom they will only retain with good food, and also because they have the revenue from highly profitable accommodation to subsidise their dining rooms, they are bound to serve better food. Such a discussion is probably never resolvable because equally excellent food (and equally poor food) can and is produced in both hotels and restaurants. The debate however highlights the undeniable connection between hotels and gastronomy — or the pleasure of eating good food. Any history of a nation's hotels therefore must concern itself with the history of the food of that nation.

Whilst it is true that hotels develop mainly as a result of economic changes such as improved transport — the railways had a bigger impact than almost anything else upon hotel development — the nature of hotels is also strongly influenced by social factors such as the type of people using hotels and how they spend their money, And obviously of major importance, because people using hotels have to eat, is the type of food they eat.

Another reason for concentrating in this chapter on the food eaten in Britain is that most people considering careers in hotels will be almost bound to have more than a little interest in the food hotels serve. Food after all, many hoteliers argue is what distinguishes one hotel from another.

Yet another reason is that those considering management careers in hotels will find that generally speaking success in the food and beverage side of hotels is the major hurdle to be cleared before the more senior management positions are accessible to the up and coming manager.

What then is the history of food, or gastronomy, in Britain?

Roman influence

As with so many other things in Britain we have to blame or thank the Romans because they were probably the first to introduce the pleasures of the table to Britain. The Romans who had access to most of the known world's market for ingredients, herbs, spices recipes and skills developed gastronomy to a high art and as with most things they took their culture to every part of the Empire to which they were sent. Roman cooking, in fact, was not so very different to much of what we eat today. A typical recipe from the cookery book of M. Gabius Apicius reads:

> *Fricassee of Pork with Apricots* Put in the saucepan oil, liquamen, wine, chop in dry shallot, add diced shoulder of pork cooked previously. When all this is cooked pound pepper, dried mint, cummin and dill, moisten with honey, liquamen, a little vinegar and some cooking liquor. Mix well. Bring to the boil and let it boil until done. Crumble in pastry to bind. Sprinkle with pepper to serve. From *British Gastronomy* by Gregory Houston Bowden

The Anglo Saxons

After the Romans came the Anglo Saxons and the main change was a greater reliance on locally grown herbs rather than the imported spices available to the Romans. Swine was the principal livestock reared for meat. Oxen were kept for milk and as draught animals whilst sheep were reared mainly for their wool.

The Normans

When William the Conquerer defeated Harold on Senlac Hill, he brought along with his legal system a renewed taste of the Mediterranean and also greater access once again to herbs and spices. So our ancestors' cooking for the 'better-off' in Britain reverted somewhat to what it had been under the Romans. Agriculture however, had declined and a great reliance on hunting as the main source of food meant that the diet consisted largely of game.

The fourteenth century

By the fourteenth century, the pleasures of the table were appreciated and enjoyed, at least at the Court of Richard II, who reputedly employed over two thousand cooks. A cookery book of that time showed the range of influence in British cookery with Greek wine and Zabaglione both of Mediterranean origin, featuring in recipes. Whilst these developments were taking place in the field of gastronomy hotels as we know them today had not really started to develop. The few people in the population who did travel at all were mainly the administration and the wealthier and more often than not they moved from one friendly household to the next when travelling whilst the ordinary traveller, of whom there would have been few, made use of the monasteries or of the inns.

Tudor times

It was not until the Tudor period that fruits and vegetables came into more common use. And in Elizabethan times, it is recorded, not less than thirty different salad herbs were in regular use. Only now are we starting to look again at some of the rarer salad herbs which were common in Elizabethan times.

Catherine de Medici

At about this time, the Italian peninsula made another significant contribution to gastronomy when Catherine de Medici married Henry II of France. Apart from reputedly being responsible for starting the use of the knife and fork, she introduced France to the foods of Italy which at that time, as with so many of the creative arts and skills, were the best in the world.

Catherine took with her to the Court of Henry II some of Italy's best cooks and other staff concerned with food. The consequence was a complete transformation of French Court food and whilst few of these changes came to Britain immediately they provided the basis of French cuisine, as we know it today and which has so influenced our own cuisine in later centuries.

The role of religion

Religion has always played a vital part in determining people's eating habits and this was certainly so in Puritan households where food was eaten for nourishment and not for pleasure. In fact, this tradition still persists in much of Britain today. It is only necessary to compare the proportion of household incomes spent on foods in Britain and elsewhere in Europe and also to compare the types of dishes prepared by the average housewife here, and in France for example, to see that in Britain very different attitudes to food prevail even today. In spite of the generally sombre cuisine throughout Britain, most menus consisted of little more than meats and puddings, there were occasional bright spots. Surviving recipe books of the seventeenth century show that there were people who must have viewed cooking and eating the results as a pleasure and not merely as a means of nourishment. Sir Theodore Maycore, in his *Archimagirus Anglo-Gallicus* or Excellent and Approved Recipes and Experiments in Cookery, lists some excellent recipes such as the one for London Pie. This was a pie containing:

> Marrow bones, cock sparrows, potatoes, eringo roots, lettuce, chestnuts, dates, oysters, citron rinds, artichokes, egg yolks (hard boiled), lemons, barberries, pepper, nutmeg, cinnamon, cloves, and currants. When cooked it was to be liquored with white wine, butter and sugar.
>
> From *British Gastronomy* by Gregory Houston Bowden

The eighteenth century

This century was the turning point for Gastronomy in Britain. Not only did the enjoyment of food become more accepted, but it became the height of fashion to employ French chefs. At the same time, agricultural science was forging ahead with improvements being made in vegetable growing and in the rearing of livestock. For example, potatoes had been in Britain now for well over a hundred years and their use was spreading. The end of the eighteenth century saw the French Revolution, and whilst the French, through the force of arms, spread their culture over the length and breadth of Europe, the Emigré Royalists took with them to their places of exile, their own cuisine and many of their staff as well. One consequence was the spread of French cuisine and the establishment of French restaurants in London.

Two names stand out more than most others at this time. In 1816 a great French Chef, Careme was enticed to the Royal Pavilion at Brighton to attend to the gastronomic welfare and delights of 'Prinny', the pleasure loving Prince of Wales, who was later to become George IV and who was responsible for turning the village of Brighthelmstone into the major resort town of Brighton. The second man, and the one whose name must rank with Escoffier and Ritz, was Alexis Soyer, who was Chef at the Reform Club from 1837 to 1850. Gregory Houston Bowden in his book 'British Gastronomy' goes so far as to say that because of Soyer 'good eating out in Britain began in the London Clubs'. Today still, some clubs, such as Boodles in St James's serve food which is certainly comparable to any available anywhere in the capital.

The Savoy

Soyer's cooking became sufficiently famed for other clubs to have to compete so that within a fairly short time, most gentlemen could expect to eat well at their Clubs. However, Clubs had one limitation. They could not admit ladies. Obviously this state of affairs could not be allowed to persist for long, and so when the Savoy Hotel opened in 1899 it incorporated a restaurant soon to become the first of Britain's great restaurants. For a period the Savoy boasted Cesar Ritz as manager and Auguste Escoffier as Chef, at that time probably the best hotel manager and the best Chef in the world and the fore-runners of other great hoteliers and restaurateurs trained at the Savoy or Claridges such as Sovrani Quaglino, Maretta, Donzelli and Contarini. Between them they offered standards of service and food which the world has not probably seen since. Such was their success, that other restaurants rushed to satisfy the growing demand for parties large and small, simple and sumptuous.

Hotels

Having looked briefly at the food our ancestors were eating, let us take a look at the development of hotels as a separate but closely related subject.

People have travelled from place to place for thousands of years and in their travels they have needed to find food and accommodations. In some cases, these resting places were set up by the state. In others, the Church took responsibility for providing for the traveller. The 'hospices' of France were run by religious orders, especially for travellers as were many similar establishments in Britain. Private individuals set up in business offering food and accommodation to the traveller and for his animals. These were known as inns. The word hotel, describing a place providing food and accommodation only appeared very late in our vocabulary. Even early twentieth century English language encyclopedias do not list the word hotel but use the word inn.

The Inn

Inns have always played important roles in our history and they appear regularly in our literature. Chaucer immortalised the Tabard in Canterbury Tales and Charles Dickens' Mr Pickwick, a nineteenth century gourmet, no doubt enjoyed many a meal in Inn's such as the Royal Hop Pole which to this day meets the needs of the traveller going through Tewkesbury.

In spite of there being Inns throughout the country most people, once they had arrived at their destination, stayed with friends or in rented accommodation, and the Inns continued to provide mainly for the traveller. Even today the Common Law duties of hotel keepers only apply to travellers and not to permanent residents.

Coaching Inns

Travel increased considerably during the eighteenth century and the speed and efficiency depended upon the coaching inns in the town centres and the posting houses along the way. A busy coaching inn had to provide stabling for hundreds of horses, in order to make dozens of horse changes a day — a long journey might need twenty such changes. The Inn also acted as a travel agency providing tickets for travellers, plus of course the food and accommodation for those going through.

Travel was a hazardous adventure in those days. Apart from the ever present risk of highway robbery, there were always chances of catching contagious diseases, being injured by coaches' overturning or horses running wild, or of dying of cold in, or on top of the unheated coaches. And when you arrived at your inn, the comforts were as spartan, for most travellers, as was the coach accommodation itself. Most people ate in a communal kitchen and slept in dormitories several people to a bed. Only the wealthy could afford the privilege of one of the very few private rooms.

London

In London, the situation was different. Some people had a need for more comfortable and pleasant accommodation than that provided by the staging houses. Consequently, there were a number of hotels, as we understand the word today. One of the survivors of those early hotels is Durrants in Marylebone. The early hoteliers were frequently people who had been employed 'in service' by the aristocracy. One of these early hoteliers whose name lives on in the hotel bearing his name was William Claridge. Having acquired a hotel in Brook Street, Mayfair, in the middle of the eighteenth century, he ran it to such high standards that it was patronised by the country's most celebrated people.

The influence of the railways

As the coaching inns played their part in developing the hotel trade in their day, so too did the railways make a major contribution to the next phase of hotel development. Steadily, between the 30s and 60s of the nineteenth century the railway companies linked the country with a network of lines that made most parts of the country accessible within hours rather than within days. This sounded the end of the coaching inn as an important part of the nation's communication system. But as the coaching inns had to provide for the traveller, so too did the railway companies have to ensure that their passengers could enjoy refreshment and accommodation at each end of their journey. The result was the construction of large hotels serving the major lines connecting cities. The Railway hotels such as those hotels at Euston, Paddington and Victoria were the result.

Small hotels too, providing to the needs of passengers using the less important provincial and regional lines, were built and many of these still bear the name the Railway Hotel or the Station Hotel. Between 1833 and 1863 it is estimated that passenger traffic, increased from about three million journeys in total per annum to over two hundred million on the railway alone.

Health and hotels

At the same time as the railways were creating the need for hotels, two other movements were afoot which also put their mark on British hotels. The two movements were both linked with an interest in, and concern for health. One was the growing temperance movement and the other was an increasing interest in the health improving qualities of spa water.

The Temperance Movement

The temperance movement, with its roots in the East Coast States of America, came to Britain in the first half of the nineteenth century. The initial objective was to reduce the amount of alcohol consumed. Very quickly, however, the work of Joseph Livesey of Preston resulted in the total abstinence, or teetotal movement, taking over the control of the temperance societies. In time, temperance hotels were opened, and even today, we still have temperance hotels in Britain.

Spa Water

The increasing interest in health turned people's attention to the health giving properties of spa water – which had been known for many years. And now that convenient means of travel made it possible to reach the various spas hotels were built to meet this new need. Hotels such as the Norbrech Hydro and the Peebles Hydro are survivors of that generation of hotels.

Resort hotels

Interest in coastal resorts grew too, particularly as towns like Brighton, Weymouth and Worthing were given Royal patronage. The railways once again, played their part making it possible to go from London to Brighton, spend hours in the town and return all in a day.

Hotel growth however was somewhat hindered by other factors. Most people who wished to stay in a town for more than a short time would find lodgings. The cost would have been very reasonable because capital costs, staff wages and the like would not generally have been included in the bill. A hotel's rates could not have competed because of the need to incorporate all the overhead and financial costs. It was not therefore until the number of visitors and travellers began to saturate the supply of rooms that hotels would have become reasonable propositions. This began to occur in the latter half of the nineteenth century and the last twenty five years saw the opening of the capital's greatest hotels. Within a space of a few years, hotels such as the Grand Hotel, the Metropole, the Charing Cross and many others all within a few metres of one another were competing for custom in a Britain which was at the high point of its economic and political power.

Frederick Gordon

This period also saw the foundation of the first large scale British hotel company, to be run by the legendary Frederick Gordon. Between the 1870s and the 1890s, he built up a company which owned leading hotels in places such as London, Brighton, Cannes and Monte Carlo.

The steamship

The steamship, as with all other major changes in transport methods had its influence on hotels. Ships such as those run by the Cunard and White Star lines were able to bring passengers over from America in days rather than in weeks. And these steamships were furbished to the highest standards, and staffed by many of the best chefs and restaurant managers. Consequently, they offered food and service in their top class accommodation that could only be matched by the very best hotels.

The main contribution of the steamship however, was the number of well off American tourists who came to Europe for pleasure and for business. To this day, many of our hotels rely on the American tourist as a major source of revenue although they now cross the Atlantic in hours, rather than in days.

The twentieth century

When Queen Victoria died in 1901, the scene was set for her successor Edward VII who according to his own father Prince Albert preferred good food to mental effort. He had a taste for rich foods and regularly ate twelve courses at dinner. He ate mainly in private houses but his style influenced entertainment and eating considerably so that restaurants became very fashionable at this time, and the period of the Grand Restaurants was born. There were about a dozen who could fit into this category of which about half were in hotels. The Savoy and Claridges still exist today and maintain some of the tradition of those days. The Edwardian era saw the growth of large numbers of restaurants most offering conventional Anglo French cuisine but others opened offering national or regional cooking such as the Italian restaurants and later some German restaurants.

The grill room

When eating in the Grand Restaurants, guests were expected to dress in white tie and tails, a practice which was not readily acceptable to the increasing number of people prepared and able to eat out. So the Grill Room was introduced. These were started in hotels and restaurants as an alternative to the main, and much more formal, dining rooms. They were a great success and grill rooms offering simpler food in more relaxed surroundings were opened up in increasing numbers.

The First World War

The 1914-18 war brought about many changes caused by shortages of staff and raw materials, so that when peace returned, restaurants, particularly the Grand Restaurants, were never to be quite the same again. In particular, the number of courses of a meal dropped considerably.

The provinces

Haute Cuisine outside the homes of the wealthy had been concentrated with a few rare exceptions in London so that outside London, Britain was described as an absolute desert.

The Railway Companies however, contributed to the establishment of some gastronomic oases in the provinces. In 1904 a French restaurant was opened in the Midland Hotel in Manchester, so that at the time the hotel had three national restaurants, French, German and American.

Ten years later, another French restaurant was opened in the Adelphi Hotel in Liverpool, a restaurant that was to become famous in later years. The Railway Companies opened many other excellent restaurants, and to this day, our Railway Hotels, now run by British Transport Hotels, enjoy a high reputation for food.

The Second World War

The second world war brought even more problems than the first. Staff shortages were bad enough in the first war, but in the second world war, because Italy was an enemy instead of an ally, the thousands of Italians employed in the hotels and restaurants were interned. Many of them were killed when the ship transporting them to Canada, the Arandora Star, was torpedoed and lost in the Atlantic. The loss of these hundreds of Britain's top hoteliers and restaurateurs certainly deprived Britain of many of the key staff necessary to help the recovery of the hotel and restaurant industry in the austere post war years.

Since the war, the hotel and restaurant industry has certainly seen the most far reaching changes. Whilst before the war travel, eating out and living in hotels was the privilege of the few, now the majority of the population can enjoy all these pleasures.

Ethnic restaurants

The consequences have been the emergence of vast numbers of small restaurants, bistros, wine bars, steak bars and Wimpey bars. We have also seen the widening of the range of ethnic restaurants. Before the war, restaurants were almost exclusively limited to English, French and Italian, but now we have many others including Chinese, Greek, Indian, Pakistani, Turkish and American, some of which are to be found in hotels.

The large hotel companies

Other major factors have been the tremendous growth in air travel, but most important of all has been the growth of large companies such as Trust Houses Forte, Grand Metropolitan and the brewery owned hotel companies such as Crest Hotels (Bass Charrington), Embassy Hotels (Allied Breweries) and Thistle Hotels (Scottish and Newcastle). These companies are able to bring financial resources and management expertise to hotel and catering management which is beyond the resources of the small individually owned business. Their hotels therefore are generally speaking able to offer consistent good standards of food, and service, to large numbers of people over the whole country.

Changes in education and training

At the same time, particularly in Britain, the education and training of hotel management and staff has become much more expert. About two hundred colleges throughout the country train many thousands of people annually to enter the industry so that there is a steady flow of people into the industry with many of the essential skills already acquired. Some in industry argue that there may be too much emphasis on training managers and not enough on craftsmen, but the total number being trained in any category is far short of what the industry needs to keep its 1.5 million labour force up to the mark in terms of both in quantity and quality.

The major outcome of these various trends is a greater number and variety of eating out places than ever before. Also, and many of the older generation bemoan this fact, there is a much greater commercial awareness amongst the management and staff of many establishments, particularly those owned by the larger companies.

In spite of this increased commercialisation it is probably right to say that today in Britain we have a greater variety and overall a higher standard in hotel keeping and catering (the Grand Restaurant being the possible exception) than ever before.

The organisation of an hotel

In Great Britain there are approaching 35 000 hotels with about half a million bedrooms. About half the hotels are in seaside resorts and the majority of the remainder are in London and other towns. Ninety per cent of our hotels have less than 25 rooms or less, and 60 per cent have 10 rooms or less. From this it is probably correct to say that the most typical hotel is a small seaside one. However it appears that most young people who train for skilled jobs in the hotel industry work, at least for several years, in the larger hotels and particularly in those run by the larger companies. This is for a variety of reasons but one important one is that the larger companies are able to provide training which the majority of smaller hotels are not equipped to provide. Another reason is that the larger hotels, whether run by a large company or not, are able to reduce the effects of seasonal demand for accommodation by catering for conferences, dinner dances and other similar types of functions which the smaller hotels are unable to provide for. These larger hotels are able therefore to provide the continuity of employment which is so essential during the early years of a person's career.

How is an hotel organised?

A whole variety of factors determine the precise organisation of each hotel, and it is probably safe to say that there are no two hotels with precisely the same organisation. Some hotels are very seasonal, many even close down in the winter. Other hotels are in busy city centres and cater for individual businessmen, who each stay just one or two nights. Others are in tourist centres and these hotels will cater for large parties who may stay for a night or for a week and who arrive by the coach load. Yet others specialise in conference business and these have to be expert at catering for very large numbers in very short periods of time.

Other factors too influence the organisation of an hotel. If trade is constant and it is possible to recruit skilled staff the hotel will

1 Organisation chart of a large hotel
The Maidenhead Eurocrest

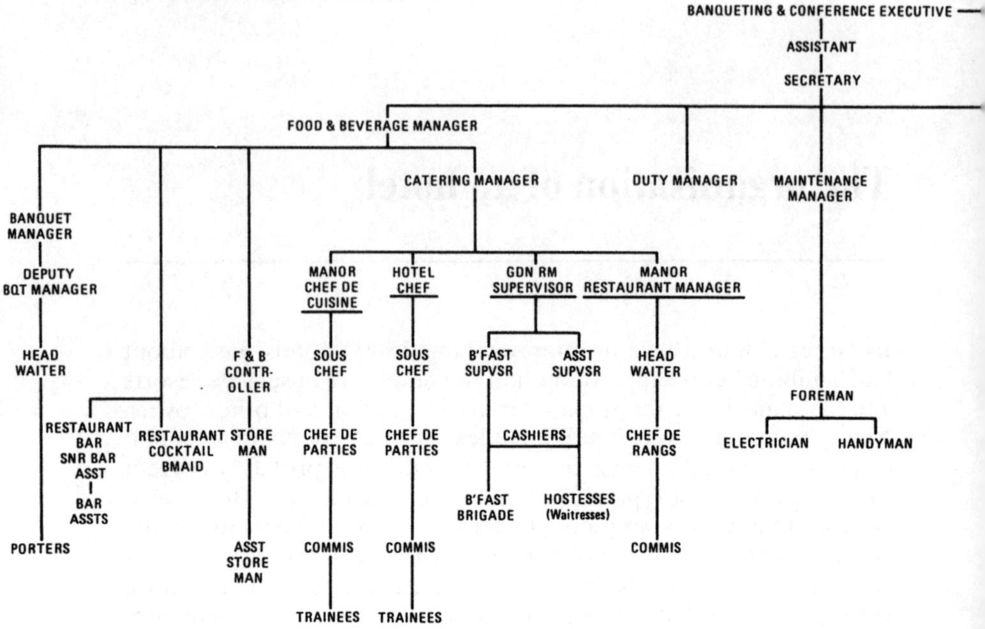

have a high proportion of 'full-time' staff. On the other hand if trade fluctuates a great deal the management will try to rely upon a team of 'part-timers', that is, staff who come only when they are needed thus saving the company paying wages to staff who may have little or no work to do.

All of these factors, plus many more, such as the managements own particular views on hotel organisation, will each influence the numbers and type of staff which will be employed in each hotel.

Therefore it is not possible to say that there is a typical hotel organisation. In order however to illustrate the types of organisation and the different types of jobs which can exist in hotels two different types of hotel are illustrated. One is the busy city type hotel which can cater for most types of trade including businessmen, tourists, and conferences. The other is a small twenty bedroomed hotel catering for individual businessmen and family holidays. These two hotel organisation charts shown in figures 1 and 2, will illustrate the differences between large and small hotels and particularly how the staff in smaller hotels need to be very versatile compared to their 'big hotel' colleagues who need, instead, to be extremely quick and efficient in their narrower but more intensive field.

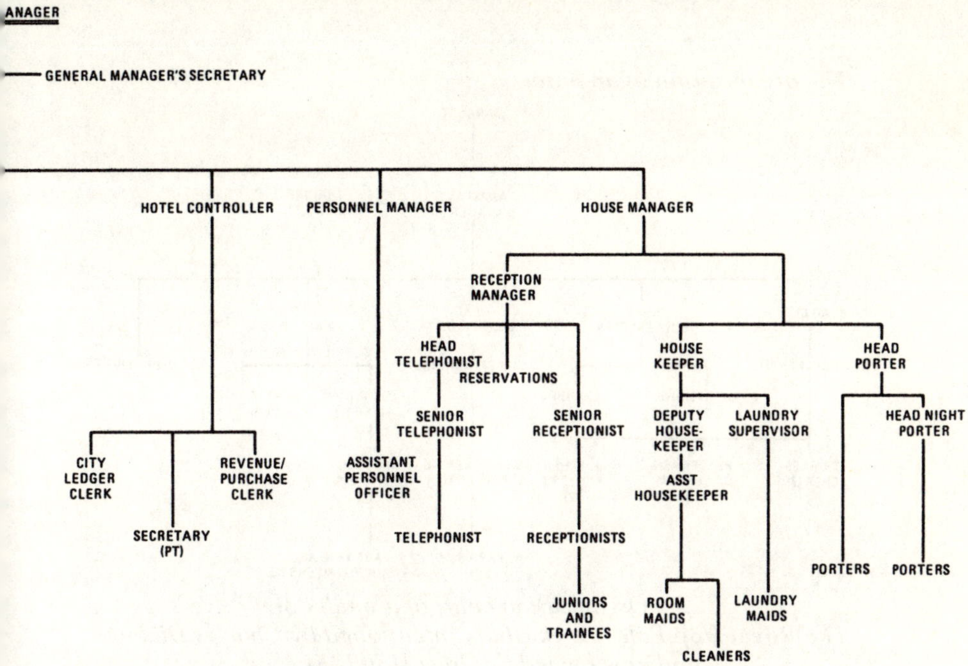

What is a five star hotel?

Neither of these charts, however, can show the full range of services which can be provided by hotels today. Figures 3 to 7 shows a comprehensive list of services and the staff which might be employed to provide these services within today's modern hotel industry. The number of different services a hotel offers its guests normally determines the number of stars, or classification, which a hotel is awarded by one of the motoring organisations who have taken it upon themselves to classify hotels.

Some hotels, which provide a very comprehensive range of services are awarded five stars, whilst at the other extreme are those hotels who provide very basic facilities and are awarded only one star or they may not even qualify for a star at all. The system of classification is criticised by many because it indicates the range of service rather than the quality of service. For example the number of bedrooms with bathroom is of greater importance in determining star rating than the quality of the restaurant food. Hotel classification however is very important within the industry because it is directly related to the 'market' or type of customer the hotel will be setting out to cater for. A five star hotel will be catering mainly for people where quality may be of greater importance than the price whereas the three star hotel will be catering for

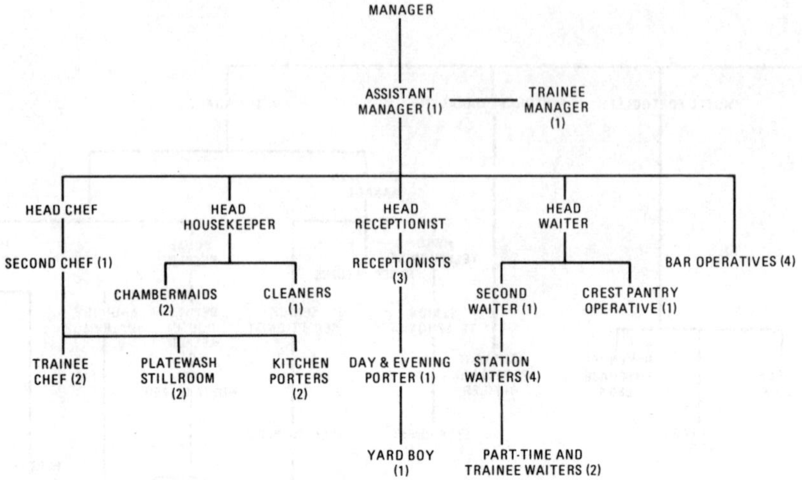

2 Organisation chart of a small hotel
The Royal Hop Pole, Tewkesbury, mentioned by Charles Dickens and now owned by Crest Hotels Europe

those whose budgets are more limited. The standards in a five star or de luxe hotel are usually of an international level, that is comparable to the standards in the best hotels throughout the world. Having said that it is important to bear in mind however that there are some top class hotels which themselves do not wish to be classified by the motoring organisations feeling that their own reputation is enough to bring guests to their door. The food served in hotels however is graded differently. A whole variety of people and organisations such as Egon Ronay and the Automobile Association set out to offer guidance on the quality of food served by a hotel or restaurant and these accolades are eagerly sought by hoteliers and restaurateurs.

From the point of view of someone considering a career in the hotel industry however such classification schemes are of importance because at some stage in your career you would have to make up your mind as to which type of hotel or hotel company you would wish to work in. Some may feel that to work in the de luxe hotels, providing the best of everything to the wealthy and the famous is their ambition. Undoubtedly many will find the glamour of the top class hotels attractive but it is important to recognise that the glamour itself is very temporary and that behind all the glamour is a great deal of hard work, long hours and intensive training. Others will feel that they will get more satisfaction out of providing more modest services to the everyday businessman and holiday-maker. As a general rule, however, most people who are entering the hotel world are advised to go for a basic training which will show them the best possible standards of service. As an example, it is generally easier for a chef who has trained in a first class kitchen to adjust to more modest standards (which may be commercially more rewarding) than for a chef who has trained in 'popular catering' to adapt his standards to those set by a top class restaurant.

Whatever the type of hotel you choose to work in its aim is to satisfy the needs of its guests. These may be, in a de luxe hotel, of the most demanding and often by normal standards extravagant. Alternatively the guests' requirements may be of the most modest and simple. In either case however it is a hotel's function to meet its guests' needs and if you become part of this world this is what your work will be all about.

Uniformed staff

On entering most large hotels the first person you are likely to meet is one of the members of the hall porter's department. To most people, including hotel guests, there may appear to be little difference between the various staff in the first class hotel foyer, most will be wearing colourful uniforms which have their origins in the days of liveried servants and horsedrawn coaches.

The hall porters' department however has a considerable range of responsibilities, which in the larger top class hotels will be divided amongst a whole team of porters.

Hall porters claim that they, more than any other single department are responsible for making a guest's life an easier one, whilst the guest is in the hotel and even after he has left it. It is to this department that the guest turns, (and frequently the other hotel departments as well), when something ordinary like a theatre ticket or a taxi is needed, or when something extraordinary is required.

The hall porter's responsibilites

As with so many jobs in an hotel, the size will determine the exact nature of the duties performed by its staff. In a large hotel the head hall porter's role is largely supervisory, organising the work of many subordinates. In a small hotel the hall porter may be the only one to do most of the duties normally carried out by hall porters. In either case, however, the hall porter is responsible, amongst other things, for greeting guests, helping them with their luggage, answering their queries, recommending entertainment, selling or obtaining tickets, organising transport, dealing with guests' mail both when guests are in the hotel and before they arrive and after they leave, operating lifts and often the telephone switchboards, and providing valet services. And at night the night porter will serve drinks and snacks after the bars and restaurants are closed and on top of all that he is often responsible for the security and safety of everyone in the hotel, checking the hotel regularly and frequently for unwanted intruders and fire.

Figure 3 shows the range of duties which may be performed by the hall porter's department and the different staff in the department who may carry out these duties.

In the smaller hotels where hall porters are employed there may be one on duty at a time and he will need to perform many of these himself. In the larger hotels however there will be a team of people all with their specialised duties and tasks.

It is in one of these larger hotels that someone planning to make a career in the hall porter's department should start his training. The work can be very demanding because of the wide variety of areas it covers and also because, as in most hotel work there will be peaks when it appears that everyone in the hotel wants attention at the same time. Any one considering this department therefore will need to be quick mentally with an aptitude for languages and competent in arithmetic. It should go without saying that one also needs to be very fit physically because some of the work such as carrying guests cases is physically hard but more importantly a hall porter can never expect to sit down once during his turn of duty.

Training to be an Hotel Porter

The normal starting point for someone in this department is page-boy. These young men are employed initially to act as messengers for guests and for other hotel staff. No formal educational qualifications are insisted upon.

After a period as page boy you could expect to move on to one of the other jobs in the department and over a period of years you would expect to perform most duties which are the hall porter's responsibility.

Then one day with perseverence, and above all else a personality which has impressed both hotel guests and the hotel management you may be offered the head hall porters position. With this position goes considerable prestige in the hotel hierarchy. It is to the head porter that guests and management will turn with their most difficult requests and problems. The head hall porter has considerable influence in the hotel often being treated as the 'confidant' of guests so that he knows a great deal about guests' likes and dislikes and also a great deal about how the various departments are satisfying, or not satisfying, the hotel's guests. In

3 Uniformed Staff Examples of Staff and Duties
(NB Each employer organises the staff and their duties in a way suited to that organisation. The list below is an example and not definitive.)

Jobs	*Duties*
Linkmen	Greeting guests, arranging taxis, helping with luggage, parking cars
Pageboys	Running message for guests and hotel management
Lift attendants	Operating lifts, helping with luggage
Valets	Packing and unpacking cases, cleaning, repairing and pressing clothes and cleaning shoes
Cloakroom attendants	Safe guarding of guests' clothes and hand luggage
Hall porters and Enquiry clerks	Dealing with guests' queries and requests for tickets and reservations for entertainment, travel, etc
	Dealing with guests' mail, room keys, lost property
	Taking orders for early calls, tea, breakfasts, snacks
	Operating telephone switchboard
	Additional duties performed by departmental staff include:
	Hotel Security covering thefts, fires, etc
	Cleaning of Public Areas 'Setting up' and clearing function rooms
Head porters	Dealing with VIPs Organising staff rosters Training staff Health and safety matters

addition to this, because he arranges things like taxis, entertainment, and restaurant reservations he is sought out and wooed by night club and restaurant managers who attempt to ensure that he will favour them when he has to advise his guests.

Depending upon the size and standing of the hotel the head hall porter may be eligible to become a member of the *Societé des Clefs d'Or,* the international society of the head hall porters of the world's better hotels, which is the final accolade and ambition of most aspiring hall porters.

EPTION
JANUARY
FEBRUARY
MARCH
APRIL
1976
FRAMES
1976
JUNE
JULY
AUGUST
NOVEMBER
DECEMBER

CUSENIER

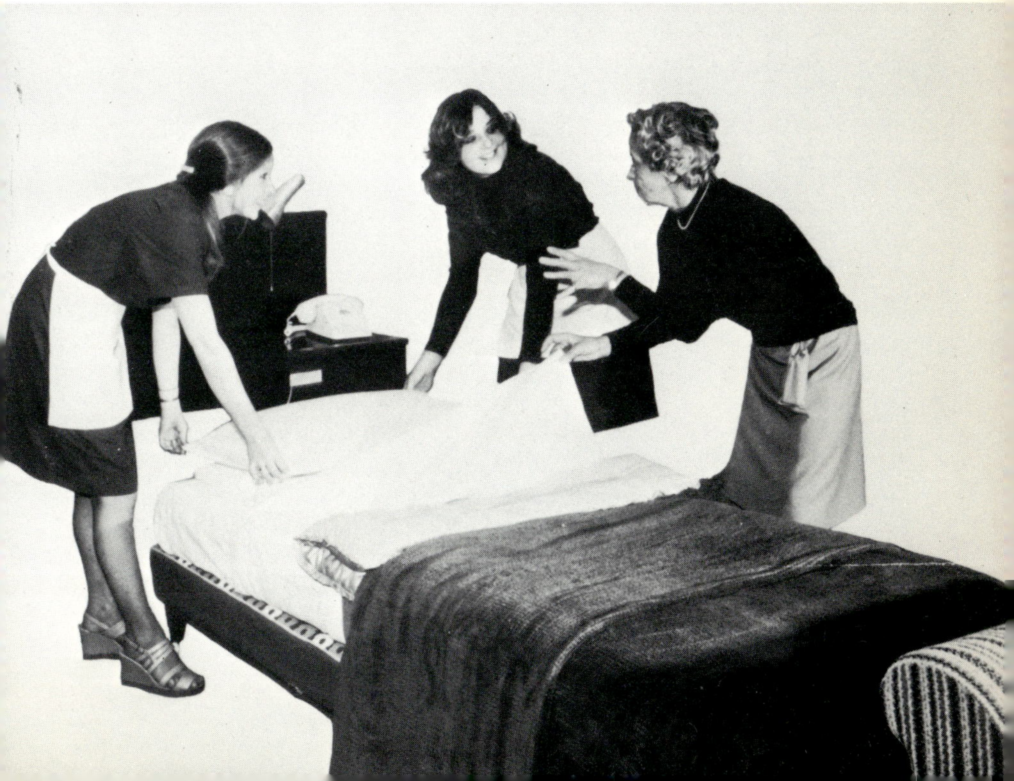

Front office and reception

In the last chapter the hall porter's department was considered which is a department that is becoming more and more the special preserve of the larger and top quality hotels. Whilst the number of hall porters in the industry may not have declined in absolute terms as a proportion of the total numbers now employed in the industry they are certainly a smaller group, with many of the lower classified hotels trying to reduce their need for the services of hall porters.

In the case of receptionists and other front office staff however this is certainly not the case. As in most industries the numbers of administrative staff is always on the increase and this is no more so than in the larger organisations whose need for more precise and prompt information to help them in marketing plans, cash flow management and the like creates a constantly growing need for more administrative staff. The front office meets this need as well as looking after the letting of bedrooms and certain other services. The receptionists greet and register guests from arrival and in the best hotels they also accompany the guests to their rooms. This role together with that of greeting guests and ensuring that their stay in the hotel is smoothly organised puts the front office and reception at the hub of every hotel's activities.

Responsibilities of the front office and reception

The department is responsible initially for ensuring that as many as possible of the hotel's rooms are let each night, in the most efficient way and on the most favourable terms. For example if a hotel has one hundred bedrooms each with double or twin beds the receptionists aim is to fill the hotel with two hundred guests. Obviously this is rarely possible but receptionists have to use their judgement when letting rooms because they may let a room for single occupation when there is still a chance that it could be let for double occupation.

Front office and reception

In addition because of the number of guests who book rooms and then do not turn up it is normal practice in many hotels to 'over-book' slightly knowing that usually a few guests will not turn up. To know by how many to overbook is a very skilled exercise, as unfortunately is dealing with guests when everyone turns up and there are not enough bedrooms for all the guests with bookings.

4 Front Office and Reception – Examples of Staff and Duties

Staff	*Duties*
Advance reservation clerks	Dealing with advance reservation enquiries and correspondence Allocating rooms
Receptionists	Greeting the guests and registering them into the hotel Clerical work such as filing, allocating rooms Dealing with safe deposits Issuing keys and key cards to guests Dealing with lost property Typing correspondence Use of the switchboards and telex Taking bookings for early morning teas etc. Dealing with complaints and queries
Cashier	Maintaining guest accounts Preparing and presenting guest accounts Summarising hotel accounts and preparing revenue for banking Book keeping Head Office returns Typing invoices and correspondence Dealing with customer queries
Head receptionist	Sales of Hotel accommodation Dealing with VIPs Dealing with customer complaints Organising staff rosters Training staff Health and safety matters.

Telephone reservations and guest registration

The first task therefore of the front office is advance reservations. After this receptionists are responsible for allocating rooms, greeting and registering guests into the hotel. This part of the receptionist's job is vital. It is the initial greeting and treatment that determine's a guest's opinions and attitudes about the hotel and its staff. He may arrive cheerful or miserable but it is the receptionist's way of attending to the guest that often decides whether he leaves the reception desk cheerful or miserable. If he leaves cheerful he will see the other departments in a cheerful light, if, on the other hand he leaves the reception desk disgruntled over his treatment there he will probably anticipate the same treatment from the other departments and he may treat the other hotel staff accordingly.

Apart from looking after the guests courteously, the administrative side of guest registration has to be attended to very carefully. Correct registration ensures that guests are allocated and directed to the correct rooms, that any charges they incur in the hotel are entered on the correct account and also, and more dramatically, if there is a fire or other emergency, that a correct role call of all hotel guests can be made to ensure that none has been left in the hotel.

Guest accounts

Of course nearly everything a hotel guest eats, drinks or uses has to be paid for and it is the front office that keeps a record of everything a guest consumes or uses. This includes the accommodation and a whole variety of other items such as restaurant meals, breakfast taken in the room, newspapers, drinks in the bar, telephone calls and even money paid out by the hotel on the guest's behalf such as taxi fares. All of these items have to be charged accurately and promptly because guests do not wish to be kept waiting in the morning whilst hotel staff spend time collecting information from all over the hotel, or correcting errors because of inaccurate work in the first place.

Today in all larger hotels much of the accounting work is mechanised and often computerised which helps to make the work quicker and more accurate. In the smaller hotels however a manual system called the tabular ledger is used.

Finally the receptionists, or in the largest hotels, specialist cashiers will prepare and present the account for payment to the guest. Even taking payment nowadays is no simple matter. Payment may be made in foreign currency or by foreign travellers cheque so the current conversion rates need to be known and kept at hand. In many hotels the profits from currency conversion go to the hotel but in a few of the smaller ones (and in some of the larger hotels without the managements knowledge) the profits of currency conversion go to the reception or other front office staff. Payment also can be made by one of the many credit cards and most of these have special arrangements which must be adhered to. Many guests nowadays will pay by cheque and in this case the hotel company will have its own regulations which have to be adhered to also. Finally there are a whole variety of credit arrangements and discounts which are negotiated with various organisations including normal commercial companies, 'package' tour operators, airlines, travel agencies and hotel booking agencies. All the special terms and procedures will need to be known if accounts are to be prepared properly and if the front office staff are not to stay up all night, every night trying to balance the books, or the accounting machine, a chore that has been faced many times by every experienced member of a hotel's front office.

Every guest likes to think that the hotel staff consider him rather special so many hotels, particularly the top class ones, maintain records of guests' likes and dislikes. These records contain a whole variety of information about individual guests and they ensure that many of a guest's personal foibles are anticipated and catered for even before the guest arrives in the hotel.

Apart from dealing with the reservation of guests, their room allocation and reception and the charging of guest accounts a whole variety of other administrative work has to be done in the hotel. All revenue has to be recorded and money and cheques banked. Credit accounts have to be sent out and 'slow payers' chased up. Wages have to be paid and all of a hotel's purchase have to be recorded, invoices checked and payment arranged. Statutory returns for such things as Value Added Tax and Industrial Training Levy have to be prepared. In some hotels and companies these duties will fall to specialised departments in the hotel or at head office. In the smaller and medium sized hotel however the reception staff often take on these responsibilities as well as acting as accounts' clerk, purchases' ledger clerk, manager's secretary, telephonist, relief barmaid, deputy manager, etc, all of which goes to making the front office job a more interesting and challenging one. It is probably in this department, particularly in smaller hotels, more than in any other, that no day is like another.

For many people considering a career in hotels the front office and reception hold most appeal because of the 'glamour'. Receptionists meet and attend, on a personal basis, to all of the hotel's guests including the rich and the famous. Figure 4 gives examples of the range of duties and staff of an average hotel front office. Also, because the front office is at the hub of things in a hotel, the department's staff learn more about the running of a hotel than in any other job apart of course from management itself. Consequently it is ideal preparation for promotion to bigger and better jobs, And with languages, as with most other hotel jobs, the world is one's oyster.

Every guest is a VIP

Front office and reception make special demands on its staff however. Whereas in some other departments creativity and showmanship may be at a premium in front office and reception, accuracy, patience and diplomacy are the vital personal ingredients. The ability to cope with a whole variety of requests, problems and complaints, whilst under pressure is absolutely vital. At peak times, usually after breakfast as a cashier or receptionist you may have to 'check out' dozens of people, dealing with their queries on their accounts and their different methods of payment. In the evening, the other peak time occurs, and you will have to deal with the guests arriving. Some of these will be quite simple to look after whilst others will present all sorts of problems which have to be resolved promptly and patiently. Some guests will be part of an inclusive tour (the industry's description of a package tour') and they will arrive by the coach load. The temptation is to treat them like a coach load, but everyone in the party is an individual and wishes to be treated as an individual. Other guests may not speak English and a member of staff who speaks their language will have to be found. Yet others will turn up late only to find their room has already been released and these will somehow or other have to be found accommodation sometimes in another hotel. Then a few may have simple, or not so simple problems for you to sort out, such as not being able to find their room or complaining that the shower or television set does not work. All of these things together with a myriad others test every receptionist's patience, tact and ingenuity every day he or she is on duty.

Accuracy is essential

The work demands accuracy in arithmetic and also in the correct use of language. It demands tidiness and attention to detail. Without these personal characteristics it is not possible to be a success in a hotel's front office and reception.

Apart obviously from a genuine interest in looking after people, you will need to show that you are proficient in English and Arithmetic. Aptitude in other languages would be a distinct advantage.

Training for front office and reception work

The ideal way to prepare for a career in hotel front office and reception work is to do a one year full time course in a technical college. This will lead normally to the City and Guilds of London Institute 709 Hotel Reception Certificate. To qualify for this course you should have 'O' levels or CSE grade 2 passes in English and Arithmetic.

In some cases this course is offered on a block-release basis which means that you would be combining your college training with experience in the industry.

Once you have completed this course you would then expect to join the reception department of a reputable hotel as a trainee. This initial period of 'industrial' training may take a few weeks or even a few months depending upon such factors as the complexity of the particular hotel's systems, the adequacy of the trainers and the training scheme and of course your own aptitude and attitude to the work. During your training period you should obtain experience in all the main departments of front office. Once your training is completed you would be promoted to one of receptionist. After this depending again on many factors you could move across to a cashier's post. After you have proved yourself competent to handle most of the problems that a receptionist or cashier has to handle you could look forward to promotion to a senior receptionist's or cashier's position and then onto shift leader or using the French term *chef de brigade*. The next step in the hierarchy is front office manager. After this one moves onto the mainstream of management and you could become the assistant manager responsible for accommodation.

If you have ambitions to move as quickly as possible into supervisory positions then two other courses are available. It is possible to do the Ordinary National Diploma in Hotel and Catering Operations. This is a two year course and gives one a much broader knowledge of the hotel business including all the main departments of a hotel. In addition to this some colleges offer a two year

Ordinary National Diploma in Business Studies linked with Hotel Reception.

In addition to these courses the National Examination Board in Supervisory Studies offers an advanced course for supervisors and potential supervisors. The course is normally only open to people with work experience who are over 21 and who hold a City and Guilds Certificate.

Prospects in front office and reception work must be as good as any in the Hotel industry and are probably as good as any in the country. The need for hotel accommodation is growing again and whilst much of the new type of accommodation will economise on other work in the hotel such as portering services and even catering services, people will still need to be booked into the hotel, and their accounts prepared and collected. In this area of hotel work the prospects must be better than most and because of the insight it gives into the whole operation of a hotel it opens up prospects for promotion into the mainstream of management itself.

Housekeeping

The front office and reception department which we have looked at in the last chapter is very concerned with the administration and organisation of guests' arrivals and accounts. Receptionists in their way find and create work for all the other departments of the hotel and no more so than for housekeeping. It is the housekeeping department which is responsible for keeping the whole hotel, apart usually from the kitchens and one or two other specialised areas, clean and tidy. In the largest hotels, which are comparable in size to a small town this is no mean task particularly when one considers that in many of the largest hotels a large proportion of guests stay for only one or two nights. In addition many guests make much more mess than would be tolerated in their own homes.

In the smallest hotels the scale of work and the expertise needed is not so very different to that expected of a very busy and competent housewife. She would however normally expect help from others in most of the cleaning chores. In many of these smaller hotels, in fact, the housekeeping duties are often the responsibility of the manager's wife. In larger hotels, however, the scale and complexity of the job nowadays calls for considerable expertise and a good proportion of most hotel courses is devoted to equipping the modern hotel supervisors and managers with knowledge of furnishings and fabrics, and the most appropriate cleaning methods and materials. One error in the choice of cleaning materials could result in thousands of pounds worth of damage being done to synthetic flooring, furnishings or fabrics. Or the choice of a bath cleaner which is too abrasive could result in the shine being taken permanently off hundreds of baths.

There is another development also in hotels today which is making the housekeeping function even more complex. This is the growth of 'in-house' laundries. At one time these were confined to only a few hotels in the country but with the fairly recent growth in the number of large hotels in which 'in-house' laundries are viable there are many more housekeeping departments in which most of the hotel's laundry and sometimes dry-cleaning as well is carried out.

The full range of responsibilities of the housekeeping department can be considerable and figure 5 illustrates many of these duties.

Responsibilities of the housekeeping department

However a hotel's head housekeeper will be responsible for most of the cleaning in the hotel. This will include all the bedrooms, bathrooms and corridors. It may also include many of the 'public' areas such as hotel foyers, cocktail bars and restaurants. The precise division of these areas depends upon each hotel, some being the responsibility of the staff of a particular department.

Exactly how cleaning responsibilities are allocated will depend upon the supervision and management in each hotel. In some hotels each department's staff will be responsible for the cleaning of its own department. For example waiting staff will be responsible for the restaurant and bar staff for the bars. In others however the housekeeping staff may be responsible for all departments. In one case at least even the kitchen cleanliness and hygiene is the responsibility of the housekeeping department, considered by many to be a most unusual arrangement.

Linen

Housekeeping is also responsible for all linen arrangements in the hotel. This includes storage, issuing, replacement and repair. Some of these tasks may be performed in the hotel whilst others will be dealt with outside. The largest hotels today, as said earlier, find it worthwhile to do most of their laundry and linen maintenance themselves.

Most departments in the hotel use linen in some form or another. Bedrooms need sheets, towels, bathmats, blankets, counterpanes and a variety of other linen. Restaurants and banquetting suites need tablecloths, serviettes and waiters' cloths. Bars need bar mats and linen for drying glasses. Lounges may need antimacassars (rare today) and tray cloths. Kitchens will need chefs' whites (their protective clothing) and kitchen cloths. And front office and the hall porters will need their uniforms. Apart from these, guests, management and staff all have their personal laundry and dry cleaning needs which will fall to the housekeeping department to attend to.

A variety of services

In the top hotels where a valet service is provided this may well fall to the housekeeper to supervise. In the larger hotels which can afford to employ a florist or even a florists' department the housekeeper may be responsible for this as well. In smaller hotels on the other hand the housekeeper will often be responsible for the floral arrangements herself. Likewise in smaller hotels the housekeeper is often the most senior woman in the hotel so she often has to be the 'female staff' personnel officer. In addition she is frequently responsible for supervising the staff accommodation.

There are of course two other jobs which require skill and knowledge beyond that of the normal housewife's. These are the laundrymaid's and the linenmaid's. If however someone wished to specialise in this type of work it may be better to obtain experience outside of hotels, for example with a laundry firm where the range of experience is likely to be wider.

A housekeeper's work

Many hotel guests see only their bedrooms and the hotel foyer and corridors so they can judge the standards of the hotel only by the work of the housekeeping department. Housekeepers therefore make a vital contribution to the profits and the reputation of the hotel. A housekeeper consequently has to have uncompromisingly high standards of cleanliness, hygiene and tidiness. Her work has to be completed according to strict 'release' times, that is times by which reception need the rooms to let them again, so the ability to organise her own, and others' work is vital. The housekeeper is responsible for large stocks of expensive linen, cleaning materials, and often early morning tea and breakfast supplies, all of which have to be strictly controlled and accounted for. Many of these supplies are attractive to guests and staff alike and are liable to be pilferred if not strictly controlled. The housekeeper needs therefore to be methodical and systematic. At the same time she is expected to work with much less customer contact than most other departmental heads because much of a housekeeper's work is behind the scenes. She comes into contact with guests less frequently than do many other hotel staff, and when she does it is often because something may have dissatisfied a guest. Maybe a shower is not working correctly, maybe a towel is missing or maybe a guest has had something stolen from his room. So a housekeeper needs to be as tactful and patient as any other member of the hotel staff, but she must be more prepared to work without the constant contact with guests which make's so many of the other jobs in a hotel so rewarding.

A housekeeper's training

There are two principal courses that aspiring housekeepers can follow. Firstly there is the City and Guilds of London Institute 708 Housekeeping Certificate. This is a day release course. Some colleges also offer it on a one year full time or block release basis. Ideally, if you are planning a career in housekeeping you should combine or follow your course with training in a hotel that is large enough to offer you experience in most of the duties of the housekeeping department.

After training you would normally expect to be promoted to 'floor housekeeper', that is the person who is responsible for supervising the work of the room-maids on that floor. Each room maid has a section of rooms which will vary on the standard and age of the hotel from about ten to as many as seventeen or eighteen. In some cases the room-maids look after their adjacent corridors and pantries whilst in other cases there may be corridor maids and even pantry maids. The floor houskeeper will allocate work out and will then check each room before releasing it. In order to maintain high standards some hotels run competitions for the room maids giving prizes to those with the best kept rooms. The floor housekeeper will also organise maintenance and repairs on her floor liaising as appropriate with the head housekeeper or maintenance staff. For the heavy work she may also be able to call upon house porters, who are to be distinguished from the hall porters, and who work exclusively for the housekeeping department. Depending on the amount of work to be completed the floor housekeeper may have to arrange overtime or to move maids around as they complete their own sections to help those who may be behind or who may have extra work. In medium sized and the smaller hotels there will of course not be floor housekeepers so the head housekeeper will have to perform these duties herself.

Staff	*Duties*
Room maids	Cleaning of rooms, bathrooms, corridors and pantries, washing up crockery and cutlery Testing of equipment in bedrooms, eg television sets, trouser presses, etc. Service of early teas, breakfasts
Corridor maids and cleaners	Cleaning of corridors and public rooms
Pantry maids	Preparation of early morning tea or coffee, breakfasts etc
Linen maids	Sorting, issuing and control of linen. Repair of linen
Seamstress	Repair of linen, curtains, uniforms
Laundry maids	Laundering (and sometimes dry cleaning) hotel and guests' laundry, organising linens for the laundry
House porters	Moving linen and other heavy housekeeping supplies. Heavy or difficult cleaning, light maintenance
Housekeepers	Organising work of the department. corridors, etc for tidiness and cleanliness Selection of linen, furnishing, cleaning materials, etc Interior design Floral arrangements Dealing with lost property Dealing with guest queries and complaints Organising staff rosters Training staff Health and safety matters

5 *Housekeeping — Examples of Staff and Duties*

Housekeeping

The next step, after that of floor housekeeper, could be that of assistant housekeeper or head housekeeper depending on the size of hotel or other opportunities that present themselves. An assistant head housekeeper will take on particular responsibilities which could include the supervision of the linen room and laundry and also the training of all new staff in the department. If there is no assistant housekeeper then the head housekeeper will tale on all of the supervisory duties herself.

An alternative course that can be followed, for those who may have ambitions beyond the housekeeping department, is to do one of the more general supervisory or management courses such as the Ordinary National Diploma or Higher National Diploma in hotel and catering administration. After such a course progress through to a senior post in housekeeping could be fairly rapid, given the necessary personal characteristics, and transfer over to an assistant manager's position is always a possibility. In considering this latter course however girls must bear in mind that the proportion of women in senior management positions is still relatively small although there are signs that more women are now being taken into management positions than was the case a little while ago.

Prospects for housekeepers are very good with their skills needed in a whole variety of organisations, apart from hotels, such as halls of residence, schools and hospitals. However prospects in hotels themselves are very good. With the predicted growth in tourism and in hotel accommodation not only will their be more hotel rooms to service but there should be an increase in occupancy rate as well, both factors which will increase the need for expert housekeeping.

Food and beverage departments

Today with the amount of investment being made in the various sectors of the tourist industry, together with the amount of experience and expertise being brought to bear on the industry's problems it is no surprise that there is a convergence of ideas in solving the problems which are common to different operators within the same sectors of the tourist industry. Airlines for example operate the same or very similar aircraft on competing routes, modern cruise ships offer very similar accommodation and no more so is this similarity apparent than in the design of modern hotels. The newly constructed hotels of different companies competing in the three and four star market are so similar in some respects that if you were to remove the publicity material and one or two other 'brand image' items such as carpets you could easily be in any one of half a dozen different hotel companies bedrooms.

These similarities are very much the result of economic forces which dictate that there are only so many different ways of building hotels or aircraft efficiently. The management of the companies concerned are very conscious of this and recognise that if they are to attract and retain a good share of the available market they must offer something which sets their airline, or cruise ship or hotel apart from the competition. It is in this respect that food and beverage services, that is, all the various types of meals, snacks and drinks, play their part in promoting the individuality of an hotel. For much of the history of hotels it has been their restaurants that have made particular hotels renowned. During the first half of the twentieth century famous transatlantic liners such as the Olympic, the Mauretania, the Queen Mary and the Queen Elizabeth competed for the lucrative North Atlantic business by providing standards of luxurious living which will probably never be matched again outside of a few of the world's very top hotels.

Food and beverage departments

In hotels likewise it has been the food more than anything else that has created hotel and hoteliers' reputations. The names of Cesar Ritz and Escoffier are but two of many who made their hotels and in particular the Savoy internationally famed mainly because of the standards set in their magnificent restaurants.

Today there are still hotels which can match the standards set many years ago by Escoffier, and other apostles of *Haute Cuisine*. The emphasis however has changed. No longer is travel and the use of hotels limited to a small minority of the population with ample money. Instead the majority of hotel guests are people with limited funds so that everything provided in the modern hotel is planned with people on more modest budgets in mind. One of the consequences is that no longer do modern hotels have restaurants or grill rooms providing only the best and most expensive but instead they may provide simple food from 'self-service buffets', butteries or coffee shops. For someone therefore considering a career in the food and beverage department of a hotel the range of hotels and the types and standards of food service are extensive.

Modern business technology

Another aspect which has to be considered today is that business management techniques have come into food and beverage operations as much as into any other hotel department. This is for various reasons. Firstly, as mentioned earlier it is this part of a hotel's operation which more than any other attracts and retains, or loses business. Secondly, large sums of a hotel's money are spent on food, beverages (which include all alcoholic drinks) and catering staff wages and so a great deal of money can, and is lost, by poor management and lack of control. The consequence is that the food and beverage department is one of a hotel's most demanding jobs. At the same time it is the department which will most likely lead to the top jobs in the hotel industry. Most good hotel managers are expert in the food and beverage management field and it is the Chefs in good hotels who command the industry's highest wages outside of those earned by management. Also Chefs usually carry more status in a hotel than any other head of department.

The range of duties and jobs of the food and beverage function is considerable and it is not possible in this book to be completely comprehensive However, figures 6 and 7 show the main types of jobs and duties in kitchens, and dining rooms and bars respectively.

Kitchens

Nowhere else in an hotel is the opportunity for creativity, imagination and self expression greater than in the kitchens, particularly if the hotel still holds to the traditions of *Haute Cuisine* first founded and built upon many years ago by the great French chefs such as Brillat Savarin, Escoffier and many others. It is upon the skill of the head chef that much of a hotel's reputation rests and whilst his skill is aided very much today by technological advances in food processing and production, at the final reckoning it is his skill and imagination that determines whether good food, imaginatively served comes from his kitchen. Cooking in a modern hotel today is a combination of artistic ability, practical skill and technical knowledge. A few years ago, when far fewer people were using hotels, a chef could rely on his skilled subordinates and good quality fresh ingredients to produce high standards most of the time. Today, however, vastly increased numbers of hotel users, are coming to hotels in ever greater party sizes. Today in Great Britain there are considerable numbers of establishments able to cater for large exhibitions, conferences and other social occasions such as dinner dances. Compared to a few years ago this is a considerable increase. One of the major consequences is that, in spite of the vastly increased output of skilled chefs from hotel and catering colleges hotels have increasingly had to turn to more efficient means of supply and production. This has meant a much greater use of convenience foods and also a greater use of 'pre-preparation' and blast freezing. All of these developments have made the modern chefs' job much more complex and demanding. Now, not only does he ingredients under new and previously untried conditions, but he has to have a much greater understanding of food hygiene and the other related aspects of food technology. For example, if he wishes to pre-cook and deep freeze meals for later use he must know that certain foodstuffs used conventionally, will not stand up to the freezing and re-heating process. He will need to know what substitutes can be used to produce a satisfactory result. At the same time a head chef in a large or medium sized hotel is responsible for a sizeable 'brigade' (the industry's word for the staff of a department) so he needs to be conversant with modern supervisory techniques and labour law.

Kitchen organisation

Kitchens today can be organised in a whole variety of ways, but organisations will reflect the type of *cuisine* or standard of cookery being offered by the hotel. The country's top hotels still use the 'partie' system a system of departmental specialisation reputedly perfected by Escoffier at the Savoy whilst very recently constructed hotels catering for the middle market will use a much more streamlined system relying to a great extent upon the preparation of foods, often prepared in their own central kitchen. This second method economises considerably on the use of skilled labour in several dispersed units, instead concentrating skilled labour in the central kitchens. At the same time it puts different demands upon the individual hotel chefs who have to bring a high degree of organisational ability and business expertise to their jobs in order to cope with the very large numbers, quick turnround and highly competitive margins of profit which both their company and their guests require.

Working head chefs

At the other extreme of course is the chef of a small country hotel who has to do everything himself without assistance. In such a kitchen there is no one else to do the many kitchen chores, which in a larger kitchen are delegated to kitchen porters or to the kitchen *commis*, the French expression for junior cooks. In the small kitchen, as in so many departments of small hotels, the departmental head is not only the supervisor but he or she is often also the main, source of labour. As the organisation charts of the two hotels show these various duties will be divided amongst many subordinates whilst in the small hotels many, if not all, will fall on the working chef.

The work of a kitchen

In spite of the differences between the many types of hotel kitchens, there are many similarities too. Once breakfast has been served preparation for the lunch time meal begins. Supplies will be drawn from the store and the cooks, (the title Chef is normally reserved for the head of the kitchen) start to cut these up, to fry them, to mix them to boil them or to cook these raw materials in one of the dozens of ways a skilled cook knows of preparing for the final product. Some of the work will be preparing *mis-en-place* the French word describing the raw materials and other supplies which are kept ready at hand for the time they are wanted. This process is essential if many dishes are to be cooked speedily but satisfactorily. Some of the work earlier in the day will be the preparation of dishes such as fricassees, and navarins which are special stew dishes which will take some time to cook. In the best kitchens soups will be made from fresh ingredients and these soups take much longer than those made from packets, so fresh soups will have to be put on to cook early in the day as well.

If there is a banquet that evening some of the preparation may start that morning, although most likely, much of it will have been done even earlier. The various potatoes and vegetables will have to be prepared for cooking later on, steaks and other cuts for grilling will have to be portioned and laid out on trays, if they are not purchased pre-portioned. Every last item should be thought of, even down to having salt, pepper and chopped parsley to hand, so that a guest is not kept waiting, nor a dish spoiled due to lack of forethought. As service time approaches clean plates, silver flats sauce boats and many other items, all necessary to the smooth and prompt service of a hotel meal, have to be brought into the kitchen, checked for cleanliness, and placed in hot plates which will ensure that they are at the right temperature when they are required later for service. These will come from the silver-room in the larger hotels, where thousands of pounds worth of expensive silver plate is kept. In smaller hotels the silver may be the responsibility of the kitchen porters who are responsible for all the washing up of crockery, cutlery, glassware and the saucepans and other kitchen utensils used in the course of a day. In most hotels today, apart from the smallest, washing up has been mechanised so that kitchen porters merely feed most things to be washed up into one end of a large machine which washes, sterilises and rinses everything going through it.

Kitchen French

Once service starts the tempo in the kitchen increases noticeably, the cooks may still be finishing some of their *mis-en-place* and catching up on the last minute chores. The roast joints will be checked to ensure that they are cooking at the right rate and stews will be checked and finished with additional seasoning, cream and anything else that is necessary to bring a dish up to the right standard. At about this time the first orders start to come in. In the largest kitchens, with many cooks working in the different 'parties', the noise of saucepans on stoves, steamers hissing and cooks calling to each other would prevent most people from being heard so the chef or a subordinate, maybe a *sous chef* (under chef) or an *aboyeur* (translated literally from the French 'barker') will call out the guests' orders using a loudspeaker. In most traditional kitchens, and even in modern kitchens where the staff have had a training based on the French *haute cuisine* these orders will be given in French.

The tempo will increase further as the peak time, usually between one o'clock and one thirty approaches. It is now, with noise at its highest, temperature at its hottest, and pressure for everything to be served apparently at the same time that chaos may appear to reign, at least to the outsider. It is certainly the time when tempers are at their shortest, and the kitchen staff are conviced that there is a conspiracy amongst the waiting staff to make the cooks' lives as difficult as possible. In spite of the apparent chaos however, considerable coordination and control is being exercised. Soups and starter courses come to the hot-plate, the chef's control point, when he calls for them. Main courses come from one part of the kitchen with such things as steaks cooked medium, well done or rare as the customers have requested and their accompanying vegetables come from another, almost invariably together, so that the waiter or waitress, can take out a complete course in one journey. And whilst all this is going on the pastry department will be supplying a whole variety of desserts and the larder will be ensuring that each part of the kitchen receives replacement supplies of meat, fish, *hors d'oeuvres* and many of the other basic raw materials essential to the smooth operation of a first class kitchen.

In essence this is the description of a large and traditionally organised kitchen. In many of today's kitchens, where convenience and other prepared foods are relied upon to a much greater extent many of these tasks and skills will be modified, sometimes beyond recognition. For example, soups will be reconstituted from packets, meats and fish will be purchased preportioned and often prepared for the final stage of cooking and the desserts and pastries too will come from outside suppliers. The consequence is a change in the basic kitchen organisation. Fewer skilled staff will be needed and the need for whole departments such as the larder and pastry department will be eliminated. In spite of all this the tempo of work follows similar patterns, with the slow build up to the climax occurring at each meal time.

Most people considering a career in this section of hotels, that is cookery or food preparation, generally aspire to becoming the head cook or chef and so it is this career path that will be described here and as with any skilled career, professional cookery requires a formal preparation.

A chef's training

The best way to start is to join an employer who is able to offer a training or apprenticeship scheme which is approved and registered by the Hotel and Catering Industry Training Board. Successful completion of this scheme is becoming an absolute necessity for most jobs in better hotels in Britain today. The scheme requires attendance at technical college, either on day release or block release. During the scheme two examinations have to be passed. These are the City and Guilds of London 706, 1 and 2, Cookery Certificates. No formal qualifications are necessary to start with but as with most qualifications leading to supervisory posts or which require a good standard of literacy and numeracy, proficiency in English and arithmetic is most desirable.

Once the apprenticeship is successfully completed the next move is to assistant cook, usually referred to as *commis,* in the same kitchen, or if there are no vacancies a move to another hotel or restaurant may be necessary. If a career in top class establishments is to be followed then moves to the different *parties* (French for departments of the kitchen) should be made to ensure all round experience of the many different cookery methods and techniques.

Chef de partie

After several years of such experience promotion to *chef de partie* (French for head of department) should follow. This will mean total responsibility for the running of one of the departments in the kitchen, such as the one responsible for preparing all the different vegetable dishes. In status the top *partie* is the one responsible for preparing all the sauces. This chef is known as the *chef saucier.*

Sous chef

The next step up after *chef de partie* is to *sous chef* (French for under chef) the person who is the head chef's deputy. The *sous chef* will probably take on several of the administrative tasks of the kitchen for example he may be responsible on a day to day basis for organising staff rosters and for the training of the apprentices and any new staff. Obviously he deputises for the head chef in his absence on days off, holidays and the like.

Chef de cuisine

Finally for those with the expertise and personal qualities necessary to run a kitchen comes promotion to *chef de cuisine,* the French title for the head of the kitchen. Normally no one else in an hotel carries as much status and prestige as this person. In fact in many hotels the chef is paid more than the manager himself and is frequently the most valued member of the hotel staff. Consequently head chefs, particularly those who have made a reputation for themselves can and do command the highest wages in the industry, outside of those of the industry's senior managers. For a small and select few there is one more step and this is to take charge of several kitchens in one hotel. The person in this position, who supervises maybe several head chefs, and scores of cooks and ancillary kitchen staff, is known as *le maitre chef des cuisines,* the master head of kitchens.

This is a description of a traditional route to the top, but nowadays, as in many things, promotion can come quickly, to the young and expert. In modern hotels relying on simplified means of food preparation many of these steps can be by-passed, with recently qualified cooks becoming assistant chefs. Many young people in their middle and late twenties are now in charge of kitchens serving hundreds of meals a day. It is possible furthermore for the highest of them to move across to food and beverage management thus entering the main stream of management. And where it may not be possible to become *maitre chef des cuisines* it is now a realistic hope to become catering adviser to a group of hotels, restaurants or public houses.

During this period of development a person with sights set on a top job may have to move around several hotels to gain the necessary experience. Although it is more possible today to confine such moves to one employer within a number of hotels. At the same time completion of several more courses will considerably improve the chances of getting into the top jobs. The first is the 'On Job Trainers' course. This is designed to equip people who are already skilled in their own jobs to pass on these skills effectively to others. In many cases, where hotels have registered apprentices, it is a condition that the chef is himself trained as a trainer.

The next course to be considered is the City and Guilds of London 706/3 Advanced Cookery Certificate. This course, in two parts, is designed to give much greater understanding of theoretical and practical aspects of kitchen work and so includes subjects such as kitchen lay-outs, basic principles of marketing, quality control and a variety of other subjects necessary to effective kitchen work. These subjects are combined with advanced practical work.

The personal qualities of a chef

Kitchen work, particularly at the supervisory levels, is complex making demands on a person's administrative, social and creative talents. In addition the modern approach to catering management demands a businesslike approach to what was an artistic calling. Without a combination of these abilities a successful career in kitchens today is unlikely. There are of course one or two exceptions, for example, pastry work in top hotels makes much greater demands on one's creative abilities when compared to the work of a banqueting chef, where organisational abilities will be at a premium.

Prospects

The long term career prospects in professional cookery are excellent particularly with the steady growth in tourism, more short holidays, increased business travel and conferences and the general increase in eating out. In addition when the alternative forms of employment open to trained chefs are considered such as industrial catering and hospitals, office blocks and educational establishments, schools and travel a career in food preparation must be considered a secure one. The variety available too is increasing with a greater demand for popular, value for money food, which is in turn increasing the demand for convenience type foods. And the increasing use of convenience foods is itself creating a reaction with many people now seeking out freshly prepared foods, skillfully and imaginatively cooked by skilled craftsmen.

Restaurants

The first part of this chapter has been devoted to describing the type of conditions and work someone making a career in kitchen work is likely to encounter. Obviously however it is not enough to prepare the food. Other people are needed to sell and to serve what is prepared in the kitchens. These are the food service or waiting staff, and as with the food preparation or cooking side, there have been considerable changes in recent years.

Food service staff are responsible for ensuring that a guest's requirements are communicated from the dining room to the kitchen and that the finished product is served to the guest in a satisfactory condition. In most cases this may be quite straight forward merely involving taking the order from the guests, taking the order to the kitchen and collecting the prepared food which is then served to the guest at his table. However there are many variations. Some guests in top class hotels expect service in their own suites and this puts particular stresses on the organisation, such as ensuring that the food is hot when it is served to the guest. Other guests require that their food is prepared in special ways which must be clearly understood and communicated to the kitchen. This may be simply the way a steak is to be cooked or it may involve, at the other extreme the preparation of foods in particular ethnic ways. Kosher cookery, for example, is the way orthodox Jewish people insist upon their foods being cooked. In this case, special cooks, kitchens, and other utensils are required and consequently such specialised service is confined to a few establishments only.

In more expensive restaurants the guests often like some of their dishes, such as Steak Diane to be cooked at their table, which gives the waiting staff the opportunity to show off their own skills. The range of skilled work that can be performed in the dining room by skilled staff is, in fact, quite considerable, and includes such things as carving cooked poultry and other roast meats, filleting cooked fish, peeling fresh fruits and cooking a whole range of dishes specially developed over many years for preparation in the dining room. These cooked dishes include Flambe fruit (the French for flamed or flared), Crepes Suzettes (pancakes cooked in a sauce flavoured with orange liqueurs), Steak Diane, and at the very peak of the expert waiters skills are dishes such as *Canard Sauvage a la Presse,* a gourmet's way of preparing wild duckling in a very rich and tasty sauce.

Apart from the food service itself an expert waiter needs to know how dishes are prepared, which dishes accompany others and in what order various dishes should be served. Many guests look to their waiter for advice so an expert waiter needs to know

The Carvery

Grapefruit cocktail
Melon in season
Smoked mackerel fillet
Prawn cocktail
Choice of soups

Prime Rib of Beef

Yorkshire Pudding and Horseradish sauce

Roast Leg of Lamb

and mint sauce

Leg of Pork

Seasoning and apple sauce

Cold Roast Joints

Choice of vegetables
Salads in season

Sweets from the trolley
Cheeseboard with biscuits

Coffee

8 A Simple 'Carvery' Menu
The Regent Palace, London. A Trust House, Forte Hotel

The Royal
Hop Pole Hotel
Tewkesbury

Bill of Fare

To Start

Grapefruit & Orange Cocktail
Chilled Melon
Country Pate with Gherkins & Crispbread
*Smoked Mackerel with Horseradish Cream, Walnuts & Danish Caviar
Cocktail of North Sea Prawns
Thick Kidney Soup with Port Wine
Cream of Cornish Crab Soup with Brandy
Landlords Hors d'Oeuvres

Fish

Fishermans Platter
(deep fried scampi & scallops with tartare sauce)
*Fillets of Sole Florentine
(Sole fillets on a bed of buttered spinach glazed with cheese sauce)
Trout Almandine
(panfried trout with flaked almonds & lemon juice)

Main Dishes

Saute of Beef Stroganoff
(cooked with mushrooms, onions & yoghurt)
Escalope of Veal Cordon Bleu
(Envelope of veal with ham & gruyere cheese)
*Roast Duckling with Seasoning
(served with redcurrant & apricot sauce)
Saute of Chicken Breast
(cooked with mushrooms, white wine, tarragon & finished in cream)

To End

Choice from the Trolley   Dairy Ice Cream
*Gloucestershire Pancakes with cream cheese, sultanas, lemon & brandy
Cheese board with apples & celery

Coffee with Fresh Cream and Mints
Gaelic Coffee

*Specialities

9 *Selection from a Typical Modern Restaurant Menu*
The Royal Hop Pole Hotel, Tewkesbury

much more than merely how various dishes are served. He will need to know how to compose a menu, that is, which dishes go with which, ensuring that there is a good balance between the various major components such as protein, carbohydrate fat, etc. He will be equally concerned with texture, colour and quantities and whilst his guests do not expect him to be an expert dietician his knowledge of what makes meals more attractive and appetising will ensure that he is able to assist guests in choosing meals which they will find enjoyable. This skill must not be underestimated because after all in our society most of our most memorable occasions such as weddings, birthdays and Christmas's are all accompanied by food. The expert in food service therefore is in a position to make a person's most important moments in life memorable.

Wines and food

In addition to knowing which dishes go with which a waiter should also know something about wines, and particularly which wines go best with particular foods. Some consider that wine drinking is surrounded by mystique with the consequence that many people using restaurants today are worried about looking silly in front of restaurant staff by making the wrong choice. Other guests are not at all concerned and will drink what they consider their favourite wine with anything and everything. Neither are getting the maximum pleasure out of drinking wine with food and a waiter who knows his wine and, equally importantly, who knows how to guide a guest's choice will be increasing the enjoyment of a meal out.

Types of food service

As with so many aspects of hotels today the types of food service are extensive. At the top is the restaurant offering the best of service which include's cooking dishes in the dining room at the guests' table. This is known as *gueridon* service. After this is the less complicated Silver Service restaurant where everything is prepared in the kitchen and then put onto silver flats for service onto the guests' plates in the dining room. Less complicated still is the restaurant where everything a customer has ordered is put onto the plate in the kitchen for service by the waiting staff. Such service makes limited demands on the waiting staff who may not even need any of the manual skills necessary for the two previously

White Bordeaux

Bin No.		*Vintage*
131	Cap Montagne ... ... *Medium Sweet A.C.*	—
132	Mouton Cadet Blanc, Dry ... ... *Selection Baron Philippe de Rothschild (London Bottled) A.C.*	—

White Burgundy

141	Coteaux de St. Bris... ... ... *Hedges & Butler (London Bottled) A.C.*	1976
142	Chablis Lebègue ... ... *(London Bottled) A.C.*	1974
143	Macon Villages Blanc, ... *Hedges & Butler (London Bottled) A.C.*	1973
144	Macon Clessé, Jean Thevenet ... ... *(Domaine Bottled) A.C.*	1974

Red Burgundy

151	Le Piat de Beaujolais A.C.	1976
154	Beaune ... ... *Hedges & Butler (French Bottled) A.C.*	1973/4
153	Volnay ... ... *Hedges & Butler (French Bottled) A.C.*	1972
155	Gevrey Chambertin A.C. ... ... *(French Bottled) A.C.*	1973/74
156	Nuits St. Georges A.C. ... ... *Hedges & Butler (French Bottled) A.C.*	1972

Rhine

161	Liebfraumilch, Kron Prinz QBA.	—
162	Bereich Nierstein, Kron Prinz QBA.	—
163	Liebfraumilch, Blue Nun, QBA	1973/4

10 Part of a Modern Wine List
Crest Hotels Europe

mentioned types of service. The last type of service consists of 'self-service' which can be at the opposite ends of the food service spectrum. At one extreme self-service may be the cheapest way of feeding large numbers of people quickly or it may be the best way of ensuring that large numbers of people can circulate freely, meeting one another whilst also enjoying the choicest of foods and wines. There are of course other methods of service, such as Russian and Family service, each with its own applications and advantages.

Today, with ever increasing needs for economy various combinations of the above methods are now used in a whole variety of hotels. Many three and four star hotels, for example, now offer a combination of self service and plate service for breakfast, another combination of self service and silver service for luncheon and yet another combination of silver service and gueridon service for dinner. At the same time some of these hotels will also be offering meal service in the guests' bedrooms and in their private suites whilst a whole variety of different service methods will be offered in the private function and banqueting suites.

Wine waiting

The service of wines has already been mentioned and everyone who wishes to be expert in the service of food in hotels and restaurants needs to have a good knowledge of wines. However it is an extensive field in itself and one in which there is the opportunity to specialise in the best hotels and restaurants. The wine waiter *(sommelier in French)* needs to have a comprehensive knowledge of the wines from the world's leading wine countries combined with a knowledge of liqueurs, cocktails and the many other ways in which we human beings like to take our alcohol. At the same time he needs to be expert in food service itself and will almost certainly have started his career as a waiter on the food side of the restaurant.

Waiting is a demanding job

Waiting is a demanding job because a potential waiter or waitress needs to be physically fit to withstand long hours looking after up to thirty people in a session and the work makes considerable demands on one's memory and social skills.

In compensation however the work is varied and except when a restaurant is quiet it can never be described as boring.

Training

Most people planning to make a career in food service would normally aim to become a supervisor or manager one day and so the career path such a person will expect to follow is described here. Once again the career path in top class establishments is used but this does not preclude someone opting for a career in popular type food service, or even a specialised career in something like wine waiting. Generally speaking however if one has undertaken training in the best type of service it is possible to move into simpler forms of catering operation. The reverse however is much more difficult.

Normally you would start your career in food service by joining a hotel that offers top class restaurant service including dishes prepared in the restaurant. Such a hotel should arrange for you to attend day release at technical college in order to take the City and Guilds of London 707 Food Service Certificates of which there are three. No formal educational requirements are needed but because of the need for coping with money and dealing with customers and other staff, proficiency in arithmetic and English is a distinct necessity. Additionally aptitudes for foreign languages will be a distinct advantage.

Career paths

The first job you would be given would be likely to be that of assistant (commis de rang in French) to a skilled waiter station (chef de rang in French). In the very best hotels initially you will be confined to clearing dishes away and bringing prepared dishes from the kitchen to your station waiter. Once you become practised in handling dishes and a spoon and fork for transferring food from the silver flats to the guests' plates you will be allowed to serve simpler dishes yourself. During this time you will be observing how the skilled station waiters and the head waiter prepare and serve more complex dishes until one day you will be given the opportunity to serve such dishes yourself. When the management of the restaurant is satisfied that you can cope with most dishes being served in the restaurant and that you could give guests the necessary help and advice you will probably be given a small station of tables to look after yourself. Then once you prove your competence you would be promoted to station waiter with your own full station of tables to look after.

Progress beyond this point depends to a great extent upon the type and particularly the size of restaurant you are working in. In the very best places you would move onto becoming a head waiter responsible for a number of stations, thus supervising several station waiters and their assistants. After this you could become a head waiter in charge of the whole restaurant and then Restaurant Manager. Even this description of what can happen in top hotels is brief and may vary from hotel to hotel because some will have more levels and types of waiting staff than have been mentioned here.

During this progress upwards some people will move into specialised sections of food service. Some will become wine waiters whilst others will go into floor service and will be responsible for looking after guests in their own suites or bedrooms. Yet others will move into banquetting the department responsible for looking after the many different types of private function that can be held in an hotel which will include weddings and wakes, dinner dances and balls and conferences and conventions.

In order to progress to the more senior levels it will be necessary to take several training courses. The one following the successful completion of the City and Guilds 707/1 is the City and Guilds 707/2 Advanced Serving Techniques Certificate. This course is designed mainly for those who have to prepare dishes in the restaurant, using lamp work, and it is also for head waiters and waitresses.

In addition to these two which are concerned mainly with food service one would expect to do the City and Guilds 707/3 Alcoholic Beverages Certificate, and on top of this it is likely that an employer would want head waiters and restaurant managers to have done an On Job Trainers' course which was described in the last chapter.

Prospects are very good for people who make the grade in food service, and promotion into food and beverage management could follow if a person has made a point of learning about what goes on elsewhere in the hotel.

Bars and cellars

A vital part of the vast majority of hotels is the bar, or in the case of larger hotel the bars department. It is in the bars that people relax after a hard day's work, or where they meet people socially. It may be in the bars that big business deals are born and it is in the bars that enjoyable and often memorable meals are started.

This is a highly specialised part of an hotel and is one from which few people move once they have become established. The career path is not as clearly defined as for most other jobs in hotels. People move into barwork either from other departments in the hotel or even from outside the industry itself. A good route however for anyone seriously interested in barwork would be to start as a waiter, doing the City and Guilds 707/3 Alcoholic Beverages Certificate and then moving into waiting in the bar. From this progress into the bar itself would be fairly simple. Most professional cocktail barmen aspire to becoming members of the United Kingdom Bartenders' Guild.

Personal qualities

Bar work is varied involving the preparation of the bar before service and the service of a whole range of different drinks. Some drinks such as bottled beer or spirits and mixers are simple whereas others are very complex involving the correct mixing of several different ingredients in precise quantities. More than anything else though a person planning to work in bars must like people because most people using bars, particularly if they are alone, will want to chat to the barstaff. In some cases this can be very entertaining for the barstaff. In other cases, particularly with regular customers it can become a very boring and demanding part of the job.

A good memory

A good memory is vital, as most often orders for drinks are not written down. So too is mental arithmetic as rounds of drinks have to be totted up as one dispenses them. There is little time usually to write the drinks down and then to add up the prices.

Prospects

With more people now having more leisure to spend in hotels, whether it is for an occasional evening out or for a banquet or for a conference or convention, bar staff are going to be more necessary than ever before.

Cellars

There are still a number of hotels and restaurants in the country which keep extensive stocks of rare and valuable wines. Such wines need very careful care however and the hotel cellarmen is responsible for this important and skilled task. The number of such hotels is very limited however and if these were combined with the restaurants who also need expert cellarmen the total number would probably be counted in dozens. In any event the way to make a career in Cellars would be to join one of the few hotels or restaurants still running extensive cellars and to work under the head cellarman.

During this time a keen person would expect probably to take one or two courses including those run by the Wine and Spirit Association. Obviously it would be useful to take the City and Guilds 707/3 Alcoholic Beverages Certificate which will give the aspiring cellarman knowledge of what happens to his wines once they have left his hands. Trips to wine growing districts, distillers and also to suppliers' cellars would all add to the knowledge necessary to run a cellar effectively.

Apart from the glamorous wines' side of the work is the need to look after beer, spirits and mineral waters as well, and this needs considerable knowledge about modern and traditional beer and beer raising equipment.

Cellar work is not one of the industry's glamour jobs and a cellarman in a larger hotel must be prepared to spend much of his working life underground, working shifts which match those of the food service elsewhere in the hotel. On the other hand the Head Cellarman is responsible for looking after what is almost certainly the hotel's most valuable consumable property. His work will involve advising on buying, so a good cellarman must be able to predict how young wines will turn out after a few years in the cellar. He will also have to know by what time wines must be used because wines being living organisms mature, reach their prime and then slowly die of old age. He will also have to know how the various wines should be served and which, such as the older clarets and ports have to be decanted. He may have to decide to recork old bottles and he may have to do some bottling himself of wines bought in cask. Even within the wine field however changes are occurring. More 'house' wine and carafe wine is being served and even expensive wines are now treated differently so that sediment is not the problem it was. The number of half bottles being listed has also dropped considerably.

In this chapter some attempt has been made to describe the various food and beverage operations of hotels and the changes that are still taking place, such as the trend to use more convenience foods and the reaction this is creating towards the use of more fresh materials. This is not in fact the contradiction it appears to be but is rather the result of many more people with a range of tastes and spending powers making use of the services of hotels. From a career point of view this means that the hotel industry can now offer a wider range of career choice than ever before. At one extreme are the few prestigious hotels offering the world's best in luxurious living and at the other are the many less pretentious hotels which meet the needs of the vast majority of people who, only a few years ago would never have had the opportunity of using hotels.

6 Hotel kitchen—Examples of Staff and Duties

Staff	*Duties*
Storeman	Storeage of perishable and non-perishable foods
Larder chef	Part preparation eg butchery of foodstuffs such as meat
Cooks; sauce, roast, fish, soup, vegetables, pastry, larder	Preparation of raw materials, cooking and presenting for service
Stillroom maid	Beverages such as coffee, tea
Silverman	Cleaning and security of all hotel silverware
Kitchen porter	Cleanliness and hygiene of kitchens, equipment, pots, utensils
Head chef	Menu planning
	Purchasing of materials and equipment
	Food costing, portion control
	Organising staff rosters
	Supervision of cooking
	Training staff
	Health and safety matters

Staff	*Duties*
Waiters, wine waiter	Preparation of dining room for service
	Services of foods and wines
	Cooking in the dining room of certain dishes
	Service of wines, liquers, etc
Restaurant managers, head waiters and supervisors	Taking reservations
	Greeting guests
	Allocating tables
	Supervising service
	Dealing with special queries, complaints and VIPs
	Organising staff rosters
	Training staff
	Health and safety matters
Cashier	Preparing guest accounts
	Summarising takings
	Preparing head office returns, banking, etc
Banqueting manager	Selling of banqueting accommodation. Assisting guests with their requirements
	Arranging food and beverages; conferences, exhibitions and meetings; audio visual equipment; entertainment
	Organising staff rosters
	Supervisory service
	Training staff
	Health and safety matters
Cellarman	Ordering beers, wines, spirits, tobacco, etc
	Supervisory service
	Cleaning cellar and cellar equipment
	Conditioning of draught beer
	Issuing stock to bars
Bar staff	Dispensing drinks
Lounge waiters	Serving drinks, etc to guests using the lounge

7 *Restaurant — Examples of Staff and Duties*

Management

Up to this point in this book we have looked at skilled craft careers, as well as the supervisory careers which normally follow upon these craft careers. However it is obvious that within any hotel there are also those who plan, take decisions, organise, control the work and who recruit and motivate the many different staff needed to run a modern and efficient hotel. These people are the managers. In most respects they are little different to the people they supervise. They should be prepared to work long, irregular hours. They should put themselves out for difficult people. But most of all they themselves should enjoy meeting people and they should get considerable satisfaction from knowing that they are both providing a necessary service which helps their guests to enjoy themselves and which is providing an essential ingredient to the functioning of a modern economy such as we have in Great Britain.

Responsibilities of a hotel manager

What does a modern hotel manager do? Unfortunately although this is a simple question it does not have a simple answer. It is much better to look at hotel management today as a team effort, with a general manager at the top. The degree of flexibility for individual managers and the way in which their work is organised is very dependent today upon several factors the principal of which are the type of market the hotel is in and also who owns and controls the operation of the hotel. For example, in very seasonal hotels a new management team may be recruited every year. And in those hotels run by the large hotel companies there may be more levels of management to report to and also much more advice, expertise and support available (sometimes considered interference) from head office. In many cases however the larger companies, because they know the business through and through, and because they develop their managers, are prepared and able to delegate and to leave those managers who have proved themselves competent to their own devices much more than is the case with many of the smaller and privately owned hotels.

The type of organisation structure which is quite common today in many of our larger and medium sized hotels is illustrated in figure 1 and this shows the main duties, roles and hierarchy of hotel management. Previous chapters have shown that most hotels will have departments responsible for hall porters, reception and cash, housekeeping, kitchens, restaurants and bars. The principal divisions of management therefore are designed to integrate these different departments under managers so that the different but inter-related departments work together. As a consequence therefore it is fairly common to make one assistant manager responsible for hall porters, front office and housekeeping; all these departments concerned with accommodation whose work is closely related and where co-ordinated effort is essential. Likewise the kitchens, restaurants, bars and any other departments serving food and beverages such as coffee shops and butteries will be co-ordinated and controlled by a food and beverage manager.

These are the two principal divisions. However as management becomes more demanding so assistant managers will specialise in other fields. One of the assistant managers may be responsible for recruiting and training staff and he may be known as the staff manager. Another may be made responsible for all health and safety matters and he may also be nominated the fire precautions officer. Apart from these duties, if a hotel specialises in conferences and banqueting, there will be banqueting management. And today, now that high occupancy of bedrooms and the role of other facilities in hotels is so vital, there will be sales staff who are responsible for discovering who the potential guests are and who then going out to win their custom. And at the top of all these separate but inter-related activities is the general manager whose job is to ensure that each and every department runs smoothly and makes its proper contribution to the functioning of the hotel so that no guest leaves dissatisfied.

Head office management

In the larger hotel companies there are levels of management beyond that of the hotel manager. There may be area managers, regional managers and regional directors. In addition there are the specialist managers at head office level whose role is to ensure that the 'line managers' that is those who make the decisions have the right advice and information before making decisions. These specialist managers include people who are expert in marketing and sales, personnel and training, data processing and accounting, work study and property maintainence and other of the many specialist branches of management which are so essential to the modern, successful business organisation.

In making a choice about your career you will obviously, and above most other things want to know how you would spend your average day. Is it going to be behind a desk, dealing with the day's mail? Is it going to be filling in endless forms? Is it going to be dealing with telephone queries or with suppliers, late deliveries or uncooperative shop-stewards or lack of staff or lack of sales.

With some career paths it is fairly easy to predict how most days will be spent but in no way is this possible in hotels. The only sure thing is that there is going to be plenty of variety. The day's mail will have to be dealt with. This will include queries about accommodation and room rates, or private parties and functions or maybe lost property or staff vacancies. In the smaller hotels the manager will deal with these himself.

In larger hotels the mail will have probably been sorted beforehand and all routine correspondence passed to the appropriate person to deal with leaving only the non routine matters for the manager. Some correspondence will be from people seeking work and this will have to be read to see if vacancies exist which could suit the applicant concerned, or there may be letters replying to advertisements for staff and these too will have to be looked and suitably qualified applicants invited for interview.

Some correspondence will be from guests complaining about some aspect or other of the hotel's service and decisions will have to be taken as to how best to deal with the complaint. If it appears genuine and fair then the manager in some way will have to try to put things right so that the customer is not lost permanently to the hotel or to the company. Some correspondence will be from head office, asking for explanations about aspects of the hotel's business. Maybe the occupancy is down or maybe it appears that money is being lost in the bars and head office will ask for explanations or suggest action to put these right. There will be invoices to be checked for goods supplied or for work done in the hotel and these cannot be passed for payment until they have been checked and approved.

In the hotels run by companies a variety of head office returns will have to be made every week. These will report on things like business done by each department, money owed and overdue for payment, labour turnover and training reports apart from a whole variety of other forms that are necessary for a head office to manage a group of hotels.

A manager's rounds

This is the type of desk work that the average hotel manager has to deal with but once this is done the real work of the day begins. He must do his rounds visiting departments that he feels need looking at. Some hotel managers will visit every department daily but today in the larger hotels this is becoming less possible so the manager keeps in touch by occasional visits and by frequent meetings with the hotel's heads of departments.

Department meetings

Some managers will organise meetings with individual heads of departments when the occasion merits and they will organise larger meetings of all the heads on a regular basis. At these meetings future business and present problems will be discussed and any friction between departments will be dealt with. The two main areas for friction traditionally are between the kitchen staff and the waiting staff and secondly between the reception and housekeeping.

Staff meetings

Apart from the regular meetings with heads of departments some managers and some companies insist upon regular staff consultative meetings. These are meetings at which the staff, usually through their representatives, are given the opportunity to express any grievances or other problems they may have. In addition any suggestions for improvements from the staff will be considered as well.

Discipline

Questions of discipline will have to be considered as well and any staff whom the head of departments are unable to deal with will have to be dealt with by the manager himself. In some cases this may merely be a short verbal warning but in others it may merit a final warning or even dismissal.

Purchasing and maintenance

Questions of maintenance and repairs will have to be considered and equipment or rooms requiring attention will have to be looked at and decisions taken. Quality and price of supplies will be under the manager's constant attention and meetings with suppliers and representatives will be necessary. In the hotels owned by the larger companies many supplies will be purchased through head office but in turn there will be many meetings with head office executives such as area managers and catering advisers. These will be concerned with preparing such things as budgets sales forecasts, special promotions, menus and bar price lists.

The manager is of course responsible for the cleanliness, tidiness and hygiene of his hotel so regular inspections of all parts of the hotel are a necessary part of his routine, knowing that any drop in these standards will bring customer complaints and letters from the local environmental health department which will visit his hotel from time to time.

A key part of any hotel is the catering side so the manager will devote a good part of his time to discussing menus, food supplies and prices with the food and beverage manager or the chef setting out to ensure that the hotel's food will be a credit to the hotel.

Security

Security of the hotel from petty pilferage, professional hotel thieves and worst of all, fire are part of the manager's wide range of responsibilities and will all take up some of his time.

Finally, and above else, he must meet and talk to his guests, because without this contact he will not know how his hotel is operating. Some of the meetings will be to talk about dinner dances or conferences with the organiser himself. Some meetings will be with travel agents or even the companies who organise inclusive tours such as coach companies. But as important as all these meetings are the apparently social chats which the hotel manager has with his guests at the bar, in the lounge or when passing through the restaurant. It is from these discussions that hotel managers learn if their guests using the hotel are pleased with the service or not, and if they will use the hotel again and also recommend it to friends.

Bigger and more complex hotels

The modern hotel is now a very complex organisation and there are more larger hotels than ever before. As a result no longer can one man be expected to hold all the strings together and consequently many aspects are delegated to assistant managers and heads of departments. Even so the person who wants to progress to the job of hotel manager must be very competent in all the departments he controls. He cannot however expect to be as expert as a good chef, in the kitchen, nor as expert as a skilled receptionist in operating the mechanised accounting system. In fact today, rightly or wrongly, there are many managers who do not know how to operate their hotels' accounting machinery. This is left to people who are fully trained in this particular aspect of hotel work. Even so the amount of knowledge required of the modern hotel manager is extensive covering such things as preparation and service of food and drink, purchasing and pricing, use and maintenance of textiles and cleaning materials, accountancy, marketing, personnel selection and training, building maintenance, law and a host of other subjects. This is additional to the management skills of planning organising, motivating and controlling all of which are common to any branch of management in any industry. In fact, the hotel industry's professional body, the Hotel, Catering and Institutional Management Association recognising the growing demands being placed upon modern managers in hotels and other related sectors carried out some important research which has identified what is considered to be the necessary knowledge for a modern manager, the findings are summarised in the table on page 000.

What then is the best route to follow if you want to make a career of hotel management? Today in the opinion of most of the industry's top people there is one way most likely to lead to senior management positions and this is through following a formal training scheme with one of those larger employers known to run properly organised training schemes. Normally these will be approved by the Hotel and Catering Industry Training Board. Such a course as a rule comes after a full-time course at one of the many Colleges running one of the various courses in hotel and catering management.

Ordinary and Higher National Diplomas

These courses include an Ordinary National Diploma which lasts two years and for which four 'O' levels are necessary. The next courses is the Higher National Diploma (HND) in Hotel and Catering Administration which usually takes three years. At least one 'A' level and four 'O' levels or an OND are necessary, although competition for places reduces considerably one's chances of a place if you have only the minimum.

University degrees

Beyond this is the possibility of a degree at one of the Universities or Polytechnics offering degree courses in Hotel and Catering Administration. These degree courses require a minimum of two 'A' levels or a good OND, but once again the chances of a place with the minimum requirements are not very high. The courses last three or four years depending upon where it is being run.

Membership of the Hotel, Catering and Institutional Management Association (HCIMA)

In addition to these courses it is possible to study for membership of the industry's professional body the HCIMA. This can be undertaken full time at a technical college and follows courses such as the O.N.D. It is also possible to qualify for membership of the HCIMA by following correspondence courses run by correspondence schools such as the Metropolitan College.

Personal characteristics

Apart from one of these qualifications prospective employers look for particular personal qualities, which many place above a good academic record. The industry is not a highly technological one and therefore does not require large numbers of people with exceptional levels of mental horse power but it does need people who enjoy working with and for others and who are prepared to conform to socially acceptable ways of doing things. For example, people using a restaurant, like the people who are looking after them to have clean, well cared for appearance and so people who like to demonstrate their own individuality by not having their hair cut or not keeping to time and who would object to wearing specified uniforms or protective clothing will find it hard to find a satisfying job in hotels.

Shift work and flexible hours

Likewise most hotels work over the full twenty four hours and therefore shifts for some of the staff are necessary. It is not possible consequently to knock off until your replacement has arrived or until the necessary 'change over' routines have been completed. Strict adherence to specified hours therefore is not possible so if you are a 'nine to fiver' the hotel industry is not for you. In essence therefore if you are contemplating a career in hotels, and particularly in hotel management you need not be brilliant, or even exceptional, academically. On the other hand there is no longer room at middle or senior management level for those who are 'good for nothing else'. The hotel industry is one of our major industries employing over a million people and earning considerable sums of foreign currency so it needs its full share of intelligent people. It is demanding mentally to deal daily with many different people all expecting rightly to be treated as individuals. The majority of hotel guests are easy to satisfy a few are very easy whilst a small minority are exceptionally difficult and these few can make one's days and even one's nights, difficult and uncomfortable.

Foreign workers

The fact that there are considerable numbers of overseas visitors and foreign workers puts additional strains on the patience, tact and diplomacy of the best of hotel men. Maybe it is because hoteliers need the patience of saints that many of the early hostelries were in fact in monasteries and were run by religious orders!

Self discipline

Finally the acceptance of standards of discipline, personal appearance and punctuality which are becoming less common in many other spheres of employment are prerequisites for hotel work, and whilst flexed hours are becoming common in many occupations such arrangements are difficult to operate in hotels—when work has to be performed when the guests are about.

Where to start

The best basis, or starting point, for a career in hotel management is to join one of the larger, reputable firms as a management trainee on a course which has the approval of the Hotel and Catering Industry Training Board. Such courses last up to about a year after which one is moved usually into junior management positions. Often the first step is into relief assistant management which entails filling in for the permanent assistant managers who may be away sick, on holiday or on a course. Some companies organise what they call 'shadow' relief management which means that a trainee follows an existing assistant manager around during the whole of his working day for several days or even weeks, to observe exactly what is done before he takes on responsibilities himself. The best type of scheme however is probably the type which not only gives early responsibility after the training course itself but which also incorporates spells of supervision and responsibility in the training programme.

Assistant management

Time as an assistant manager will normally last several years and will involve moving through the various specialist branches such as food and beverage, accommodation and staff management. In the largest hotels spells as head of department or deputy heads of department may also be included as the opportunities present themselves. Promotion will depend obviously upon individual talents and the ability to make and to take opportunities. Moves between hotels within one company will be a certainty for most people who are keen and determined to get on.

Your first hotel

After several years as assistant manager the opportunity will come up one day to run one's first hotel. Normally this will be a smaller hotel but the excitement of one's first hotel, and realising that one is largely responsible for its business success and entirely responsible for the welfare and well-being of everyone using it is an experience shared only by people such as naval officers receiving their first command and it is an experience that will probably not be repeated again in one's working life.

After the initial excitement life will settle into the routine of most hotels—which was described earlier in this chapter. In the smaller hotels however there are fewer subordinates to delegate to, if any, and the manager may even find himself doing duties as barman, cook and chief bottlewasher! It is for this reason, and also because quality control in hotels is difficult to teach without a sound basis of practical experience that the aspiring young hotel manager must have a good basis of practical training in the craft-work, such as cookery, which he will be responsible for supervising and sometimes providing himself, as a manager.

After the first appointment a manager will be constantly faced with the decision about his next step. Should he remain in small hotels? Should he move into larger and higher graded hotels? Should he go overseas for a spell or should he contemplate moving into head office appointments? From this point on individual temperaments and interests and ambitions and of course circum-stances will play an increasingly important part. Some people enjoy the constant contact with customers which is a daily part of the hotel manager's life and which will be forfeited on moving into the largest hotels, where the manager becomes a 'super' administrator, or into head office appointments where guests are considered as 'population aggregates' or socio-economic groupings' and less often as individual hotel guests.

What are the long term prospects?

What are the long term prospects for someone contemplating this type of career then? The first chapter of this book sets out to show that hotels, being a part of the growing tourist industry, have excellent prospects for the future. More travel, longer holidays, more leisure all add up to a need for managers and supervisors to attend to these increased leisure needs. But many of the new generations of tourists will not be in a position financially to use conventional hotels. Instead they will be opting for various forms of self catering holidays in villas, flatlets and on camping and caravanning sites.

In spite of this however the growth anticipated in Britain alone for hotel accommodation must mean a stable industry for the industry's managers. Also as various other factors, such as the steadily improving conditions of the working force, come to play a bigger part in the industry's affairs the conditions of industry's managers must also improve steadily and these facts combined with the amount of freedom and opportunity for job satisfaction that the average hotel manager enjoys must make a career in hotel management one that deserves serious consideration by anyone with the social and mental equipment for this hard but satisfying work.

Profiles

Mary, aged 19, from London, is a receptionist in a medium sized West London hotel.

Mary has five 'O' levels and speaks French. She was attracted to hotels by her mother who is in the industry and to reception work because of the opportunity for self-development this front-of-house occupation offers.

On leaving school, Mary joined Grand Metropolitan Hotels and attended Ealing Technical College where she took the City and Guilds 709 Hotel Reception Certificate on block-release.

Mary's outside interests include all forms of dancing (which she teaches) ballet, modern and tap and also dressmaking and tennis. Her ambition is to go into personnel management within the hotel and catering industry and specialise in that field.

Peter, aged 20, from London is a receptionist in a large West End Hotel.

Peter has five 'O' levels.

He chose a career in hotels because he wanted something active and interesting. He attended Waltham Forest Technical College and obtained the Ordinary National Diploma in Hotel and Catering Operations. He then joined the Trust Houses Forte Organisation.

Peter's hobbies are eating out, the theatre, football and cricket. His ambition is to be a front-of-house manager in an international hotel.

Morris, aged 19. He left school at 17 with seven CSE passes, including grade 1 in geography and mathematics. He went to work as a commis-waiter in Taunton, attending the Somerset College of Arts and Technology on day-release. He has obtained the City and Guilds 707/1 *Food Service* certificate and is now going to Weston Super Mare College to study for the 707/2 *Advanced Serving Techniques* and the 707/3 *Alcoholic Beverages* certificates.

Morris, whose hobbies are fishing and snooker, is looking forward to working on the Continent, having won a travelling scholarship in the 'Waiter of the Year' competition organised by the Cookery and Food Association and the British Hotels, Restaurants and Caterers Association.

His ultimate aim is to be a restaurant manager in the West of England. 'There is plenty of scope outside London,' he says. 'Discriminating customers can be found anywhere. It is just a matter of acquiring a reputation for good food and good service'.

Carole aged 16, from Leytonstone, London, is a trainee-waitress at the Mandeville Hotel, London.

Carole was educated at Leyton Senior High School and has two CSEs. On leaving school she wanted to lead an active life dealing with people and was advised by her Careers Officer, since she had the right personality, to follow a career in Food Service. She was accepted by Grand Metropolitan Hotels and is taking the City and Guilds 707/1 *Food Service* course on block release at Westminster College.

Carole's outside interests include swimming and dancing. She enjoys her work very much and her ambition is to have a business of her own some day.

These 4 Profiles are reproduced by courtesy of the HCITB

Katie, aged 22, is Deputy Housekeeper in 4-star 200 bedroomed hotel near London.

Katie always had an interest in hotels working during school holidays in a variety of different jobs. These included washing up, waiting, bar work and even cooking breakfasts.

After leaving Oldbury Technical School she tried her hand at farming, looking after cows and pigs.

She came back to the hotel industry by joining the Grosvenor House Hotel in Stratford upon Avon as a general assistant. This involved working in most departments including the gardens.

Katie joined her present hotel as assistant housekeeper in 1978 and was promoted to deputy housekeeper within a few months. She is responsible for supervising the work of 14 chambermaids, including checking their rooms, ordering and issuing cleaning materials and dealing with their day to day problems.

Her main satisfaction is mixing with people and as she herself says, 'making them laugh'. She would like to own her own hotel one day. Her main outside interest is riding and maintaining her 250cc Honda motorbike.

Gregory, aged 19, is Banqueting Supervisor in a 4-star 200 bed-roomed hotel, catering for functions for up to 500.

Gregory always had an interest in hotels so having obtained 6 'O' levels he went to Stratford College of Further Education where he successfully completed the 2-year Ordinary National Diploma for the hotel and catering industry.

He joined a modern 4-star hotel with 198 bedrooms and large function facilities as a general trainee. Within a short time he was promoted to banqueting supervisor.

In this capacity he is responsible once the booking has been confirmed for most aspects of organising all conferences, banquets and other functions such as weddings. He organises staff and their wages, and he is responsible for ensuring that all function rooms and bars are set up and adequately stocked for the occasion.

He enjoys the fact that for his age and experience he is given considerable responsibility. Also the work, although very hard, has a lot of variety.

Gregory hopes, one day, to own his own chain of clubs. He enjoys driving, basketball and football.

Gary, aged 23, is Head Chef of a 2-star hotel with 50 bedrooms, 1 bar, 1 restaurant and 1 small conference room.

Gary enjoyed cooking as a child and decided to make it a career.

He decided that he wanted to work straight away so he found himself a job in a nearby hotel kitchen. He realised however that to progress he should take his City and Guilds exams and so attended Henley College of Further Education in his own time and at his own expense. After 4 years, and working in 3 different hotels, he obtained his City and Guilds 706/1 and 2.

He is now responsible for 6 kitchen staff and serves between 150 and 250 meals a day.

His main satisfaction is knowing that his kitchen is running so that the customers, management and the other staff are satisfied with his work.

His hobbies include playing football, squash and golf. He is also a music lover and able to play the guitar.

John, aged 26, is Food and Beverage Manager of 3-star motor hotel with 132 bedrooms, 2 restaurants, 2 bars and function facilities for up to 400.

After taking his 'A' levels at private school John went to Blackpool for 3 years in order to obtain his Higher National Diploma for the hotel and catering industry. He then did a training scheme with Trust Houses Forte. After being promoted to duty manager he moved to Bernie Inns where he became a deputy unit manager.

In 1978 he joined the hotels group of a major brewery company.

He is now the senior assistant manager with about 45 catering staff directly responsible to him. He also deputises for the manager in his absence.

John's main satisfaction is being able to organise and run his departments smoothly.

He plays golf, squash and tennis and also enjoys running, hiking and climbing.

Further reading

Magazines

Caterer and Hotel Keeper (weekly)
Catering and Hotel Management (monthly)
Catering Times (weekly)
Hotel, Catering and Institutional Management Association Journal (monthly); Review (quarterly)

Books – fiction

Hotel, Arthur Hailey, Longmans 1974
Grand Hotel, Vicki Baum, Michael Joseph 1972

Books – non-fiction

The Savoy; The Romance of a Great Hotel, S Jackson, Muller 1964.
The Duchess of Jermyn Street, D Fielding, Eyre & Spottiswood 1964.
The Savoy Was My Oyster, P Contarini, Hale 1971.
The Golden Age of British Hotels, D Taylor & D Bush, Northwood 1974.
British Gastronomy; The Rise of Great Restaurants, G Houston Bowden, Chatto & Windus 1975.
Fortune, Fame & Folly: British hotels and catering from 1878 to 1978, Derek Taylor, Caterer and Hotelkeeper 1977.

A TECHNICAL AREAS AND UNITS

Primary / Secondary	Major Areas	Product Areas	Units
classification based on frequency of use in working situation & generality of use in major sectors.	broad divisions reflecting major areas of activity and knowledge.	divisions reflecting, where appropriate, distinctions by product	basic components of major and/or product areas.
1 Primary Areas include knowledge & skills often or sometimes used in the working situation by the majority in at least 6 out of 8 major sectors (75% or more). these criteria have been modified in respect of the following Areas and Units for reasons stated elsewhere: Legal Aspects	1 Purchase	1 Food	1 Foods as commodities 2 Purchasing of foods
		2 Liquor	1 Liquor as commodities 2 Purchasing of liquor
	2 Provision and Service	1 Food	1 Preparation, cooking and service 2 Production and service
		2 Liquor	1 Preparation 2 Service
	3 Sales	1 Food	1 Outlets 2 Menus
		2 Liquor	1 Outlets 2 Beverage lists
	4 Control	1 Food	1 Cost and control concepts 2 Control cycle 3 Measurement of performance
		2 Liquor	1 Cost and control concepts 2 Control cycle 3 Measurement of performance
	5 Premises and Facilities	1 Food	1 Preparation plant and equipment 2 Service plant and equipment
		2 Liquor	1 Service plant and equipment
		3 Accommodation I (common to all operations)	1 Buildings & services 2 Public room interiors 3 Safety and security 4 Servicing & maintenance
	6 Legal Aspects	1 Food	1 Purchasing 2 Provision & Service 3 Sales
		2 Liquor	1 Purchasing 2 Provision & service 3 Sales
		3 Accommodation I (common to all operations)	1 Premises and facilities
2 Secondary Areas include knowledge and skills often or sometimes used in the working situation by the majority in 5 out of 8, or less than 5 out of 8 major sectors (less than 75%) these criteria have been modified in respect of the following Area for reasons stated elsewhere: Science and Technology	7 Provision, Service and Sales	3 Accommodation II (sleeping accommodation)	1 Provision of rooms 2 Sales outlets & systems 3 Purchasing of requirements 4 Control 5 Legal aspects
	8 Human Nutrition	1 Food	1 Nutritive values and requirements 2 Nutrition in menus 3 Diet formulation
	9 Science and Technology	1 Food	1 Food science 2 Food microbiology 3 Food production technology
		2 Liquor	1 Science relating to minerals, beers, wines and spirits
		3 Accommodation	1 Textiles and materials science 2 Cleaning science 3 Fuel science
	10 Gastronomy	1 Food	1 Preparation and presentation 2 Cultural and social context

B MANAGEMENT AREAS AND UNITS

Primary / Secondary	Major Areas	Product Areas	Units
classification based on frequency of use in working situation & generality of use in major sectors.	broad divisions reflecting major areas of activity and knowledge.	divisions reflecting where appropriate distinctions by product.	basic components of major and/or product areas.
1 Primary Areas	1 Marketing I	0	1 Consumer orientation 2 Consumer analysis 3 Product formulation 4 Operation and monitoring
include knowledge and skills often or sometimes used in the working situation by the majority in at least 6 out of 8 major sectors (75% or more).	2 Financial I	0	1 Accounting concepts 2 Accounting for transaction 3 Budgeting 4 Analysis and interpretations 5 Accounting systems
	3 Personnel I	0	1 Human resources in the organisation 2 Personnel administration 3 Training and development 4 Industrial relations
these criteria have been modified in respect of the following Areas and Units for reasons stated elsewhere: Industry I	4 General I	0	1 Management environment 2 Policy and planning 3 Organisation 4 Information and control 5 Specialist techniques
	5 Industry I	0	1 Historical context 2 Significance 3 Structure and organisation 4 Resources 5 Sources of information
	6 Legal Aspects	0	1 Legal framework 2 Marketing and consumer aspects 3 Financial and accounting records 4 Personnel and employment
2 Secondary Areas	7 Marketing II	0	1 Marketing organisation 2 Market studies 3 Sales promotion
include knowledge and skills often or sometimes used in the working situation by the majority in 5 out of 8, or less than 5 out of 8 major sectors (less than 75%)	8 Financial II	0	1 Trial balance 2 Final accounts 3 Capital 4 Management accounting 5 Mechanisation
	9 General II	0	1 Business statistics 2 Computer studies 3 Languages
	10 Industry II (Tourism)	0	1 Nature of Tourism 2 Structure and organisation 3 Planning and Development 4 Marketing

Corpus of professional knowledge in hotel, catering and institutional services
Reproduced by courtesy of the HCIMA

Helpful organisations

Careers and Occupational Information Centre
Selkirk House, 166 High Holborn, London WC1V 6PF

City and Guilds of London Institute
76 Portland Place, London W1N 4AD

Employment Services Agency

This agency has set up a network of specialist employment offices to deal with the hotel and catering industry. These special offices are at:

3 Denmark Street, London WC2H 8LR

281 Corporation Street, Birmingham B4 7DR

8 Queen Street, Blackpool FY1 1PF

Bracken House, 14-16 Christchurch Road, Bournemouth BH1 3NF

Crown Building, Quay Road, Bridlington YO16 4LS

6 Westgate Street, Cardiff CF1 1JG

Cheylesmore, Coventry CV1 2HE

Bondgate House, 90 Bondgate, Darlington DL3 7JY

103 Waterloo Street, Glasgow G2 7RY

40 Market Place, Great Yarmouth NR30 1LT

Town Centre House, Cheltenham Parade, Harrogate HG1 1DP

Beezon Road, Kendal LA9 6BP

Westminster House, Bond Street, Leeds LS1 5BE

Graeme House, Derby Square, Liverpool L2 7SE

Argyle Road, Llandudno LL30 1DG

39-43 King Street, Manchester M2 7AT

Rede House, Corporation Road, Middlesbrough

7-12 Nelson Street, Newcastle-Upon-Tyne

Huntress Row, Scarborough

7-9 Rockingham Gate, Sheffield S1 4JD

Town Centre House, Crowtree Road, Sunderland SR1 3EW

Grove House, 2-3 Grove Place, Swansea SA1 5DH

Roebuck House, Abbey Road, Torquay TQ2 5PQ

Circuit House, St Clements Street, Truro TR1 1BX

13 Piccadilly, York YO1 1PF

Specialist advisory staff are also available in the employment offices at Aberdeen, Bognor, Brighton, Eastbourne and Inverness.
Initial application can be made at any employment office or jobcentre of the Employment Service Agency in Britain.

Hotel and Catering Industry Training Board
PO Box 18, Wembley, HA9 7AP

Hotel, Catering and Institutional Management Association
191 Trinity Road, London SW17 7HN

Local Careers Service

Local Technical Colleges, Polytechnics and Universities

Main hotel groups

Reproduced by courtesy of *Catering Times*

Arden, Cobden and Norfolk Hotels
166-8 Hagley Road, Edgbaston
Birmingham, B16 9NZ

British Transport Hotels
St Pancras Chambers, London NW1 2TU

Centre Hotels (Cranston)
23 Newman Street, London W1

Concord Hotels
Beech House, 4 Lindsay Avenue, High Wycombe
Bucks, HP12 3DR

Crest Hotels Europe
Bridge Street, Banbury, Oxfordshire

EMI Hotels and Restaurants
Victory House, Leicester Square, London WC2

Embassy Hotels, Hotels division of Allied Breweries
Station Road, Burton on Trent, Staffordshire DE14 1BZ

Grand Metropolitan Hotels
The Job Shop, 3 Marylebone Lane, London W1A 4YU

Holiday Inns of UK
128 King Henry's Road, London NW3 3ST

North Hotels
58 Cromwell Road, South Kensington, London SW7 5BZ

The Savoy Hotel, Savoy Claridge's
18 Brook's Mews, London W1Y 1LF

Reo Stakis Organisation
443 Parliamentary Road, Glasgow G4 0AE

Swallow Hotels and Restaurants
PO 35 Sunderland, Tyne and Wear

Trust Houses Forte
1 Jermyn Street, London SW1Y 4UH

Thistle Hotels and Scottish and Newcastle Hotels
33 St Mary's Street, Edinburgh EH1 1TN

Index